HAMILTON ROSBERG

THE RETURN OF THE SILVER ARROWS

THE STORY OF THE 2014 FORMULA 1 WORLD CHAMPIONSHIP

BY JAMES WATKINS

First Edition published by Large Door Press in 2014

All rights reserved.

Copyright © 2014 Large Door Press, UK

ISBN-13: 978-1505343380
ISBN-10: 1505343380

All Rights Reserved. No part of this publication may be reproduced, stored in a retrieval system, or transmitted, in any form, or by any means, electronic, mechanical, photocopying, recording or otherwise without the prior permission of the publisher and copyright holder.

THE RETURN OF THE SILVER ARROWS

1955-2014

CONTENTS

PROLOGUE 9
THE PROTAGONISTS 15
CHANGES FOR 2014 22
THE PREAMBLE 26

1. AUSTRALIAN GRAND PRIX 29
2. MALAYSIAN GRAND PRIX 39
3. BAHRAIN GRAND PRIX 49
4. CHINESE GRAND PRIX 59
5. SPANISH GRAND PRIX 69
6. MONACO GRAND PRIX 79
7. CANADIAN GRAND PRIX 89
8. AUSTRIAN GRAND PRIX 99
9. BRITISH GRAND PRIX 107
10. GERMAN GRAND PRIX 117
11. HUNGARIAN GRAND PRIX 127
12. BELGIAN GRAND PRIX 139
13. ITALIAN GRAND PRIX 149
14. SINGAPORE GRAND PRIX 159
15. JAPANESE GRAND PRIX 169
16. RUSSIAN GRAND PRIX 179
17. UNITED STATES GRAND PRIX 189
18. BRAZILIAN GRAND PRIX 199
19. ABU DHABI GRAND PRIX 209

EPILOGUE 225

PROLOGUE

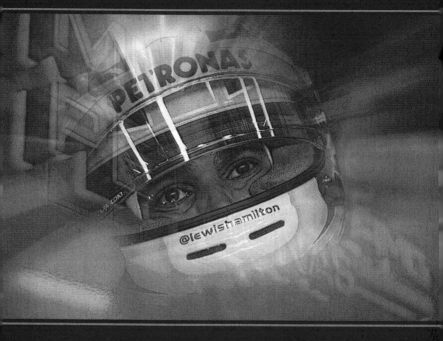

2014 F1 SEASON

PROLOGUE

2014 was always going to be a watershed season for Formula 1, with the radical changes in technology that were announced in 2011. The teams had a momentous task of instigating such huge changes, all at once, and in such a short space of time, but they succeeded in the main. The predictions of mass retirements and constant unreliability never really materialised. The surprising dominance of the Mercedes' team threatened a series of mundane processions but instead we were all enthralled and entertained by the greatest inter-team rivalry since Senna and Prost in 1988 and 1989, and maybe the best of all time, with the added spice that they were best friends in the past - and it's only been for one year so far. The story had more twists and turns than we could have expected and with the controversial double points available at the last race it was always going to go to the wire.

I remember a gloriously hot Saturday in July 1977, when, as a naive and unsuspecting 13 year old, I climbed the grassy bank on Copse Corner at Silverstone with my father and my younger brother, to be presented with that gut wrenching sound for the first time live, and they were only revving up the engines. It was the morning practice before the race. I felt the hairs on the back of my neck rise. Then, minutes later, I watched those fantastic futuristic looking cars career past me at speeds I never could have imagined, in total awe. I knew that this was my world, my sport.

My hope is that this story will entertain you as much as I am entertained by it and if you are new to Formula 1, encourage you to attend a Formula 1 event, because there is nothing more spine-tingling than seeing two technologically advanced machines battling it out wheel to wheel at over 200mph, and knowing that a human being, such as yourself, is in complete control of those machines (well, most of the time). For having driven a single seater race car around Silverstone at 130mph and realised how slow I was, while being on the seat of my pants, I truly knew what skill, daring and sheer fearlessness these drivers have and what courage it takes to risk injury and life while touching another car wheel to wheel at unimaginable speeds just to be the best and the fastest in the world. Add to this the supreme trust that you have to have with your fellow driver, that they will be fair while being firm, that they will give you space while being aggressive and you begin to understand what tremendously high levels of concentration and focus these drivers have. Then my passion was stepped up another notch, the passion I have for this amazing sport with its rich history and its immense characters, with its Hollywood glamour and with its amazing global backdrops. And wheel to wheel action is exactly what we got in 2014 and after the superlative dominance of the Red Bulls for the past 4 years it made for a welcome change.

And just as with Senna and Prost and just as with Hunt and Lauda in 1976 we had a rivalry between drivers with completely opposing approaches to their race craft. For Hunt and Senna read Lewis Hamilton. Real racers, who love the wheel to wheel close encounters and usually come out on top, with no sense of the danger or the consequences, natural born racers. For Lauda and Prost read Nico Rosberg. Intelligent and calculating, cool customers, who always do just enough to win, to outwit the opposition and to constantly work harder to better their race craft.

But not only that, we saw young drivers out to prove that they have something to give. Potential world champions of the future. Williams' Valtteri Bottas, in only his second year showed that the first race win is not that far away and who, along with Felipe Massa, gave that great marque of the 80s and 90s, a year to remember after one of their worst seasons in 2013.

Daniel Ricciardo, a star of the future, and like those great racers of years gone by, a driver not afraid to take on the big boys and beat them with style and panache and fearless overtaking. A driver who gets my vote for young driver of the year, and the best behind Hamilton, who outshone his illustrious team mate and 4 times World Champion, Sebastian Vettel. In fact he wiped the floor with him. In only his second year he achieved 3 thrilling victories in such grand settings as Spa and Canada and Hungary and included some of the best overtaking manoeuvres of the year. The remarkable ability, for one so apparently inexperienced, to put his tyres on the slippery concrete kerbs off-track in a wet race, while overtaking a driver at high speed and make it stick when most would have lost the car was truly breathtaking. And when he overtook two former World Champions in Fernando Alonso and Lewis Hamilton in Hungary over two laps, on the outside, was simple unbelievable and totally enthralling.

Undoubtedly a future World Champion and a man who brings a most refreshing and amiable character to the paddock along with a beaming smile that makes you feel okay with the world.

Daniil Kyvat, at only 19, showed some potential in an extremely uncompetitive car and secured a position for 2015 with Red Bull to partner Ricciardo. It's a move that sounds promising for the young wannabe and Red Bull do have a rather good track record in nurturing their young drivers and in making the right choices.

Finally and foremost, hats off to Lewis Hamilton, who proved he was the best all round racer and street fighter of them all. He came of age this year and I have no doubt he will prove to be one of the all-time greats of Formula 1, if he isn't already. His skill, when close racing, and his determination to be in front and to stay in front, his tenacity and ability to rise above all the bad luck that was thrown at him, speaks of a remarkably strong minded character. Prone to the doldrums at some points when Nico obviously began to get under his skin, he rose again only to be knocked back over and over during the mid-season, through no fault of his own. But he never gave up and he stepped back into the ring like a punch drunk fighter and went again, at 120%, all guns blazing and that smile after Abu Dhabi made me love him all the more. The class act of 2014 and hopefully the class act for some time to come, I believe he's on the way to being the best, most accomplished driver of this generation.

2015 and more of the same please, perhaps with the closing of the gap on the Mercedes team, which I'm sure the other teams will do, so that we have a season where more drivers will be competing for the championship. Thankfully, the ridiculous double points has been scrapped for 2015 and let's hope that no more ideas for this kind of artificial manipulation occur in the future. We've had 2014 and it was truly inspiring, but it's old hat - albeit an old hat that we really loved and like to put on again every now and then. So let's put on that hat again and relive the great moments of a great year and also let's hope that Jules Bianchi recovers from his horrendous crash in Japan and let's hope that Formula 1's governing body can learn from his accident as they so successfully did after Ayrton Senna's death in 1994. And also let's hope that the most successful World Champion this sport has ever had, recovers from his accident on the Alpine slopes, a full recovery, so that once again we can see him at a Grand Prix in the future and we can listen to the tales of his 7 World Championships and learn from the tremendous experience he has to offer. And finally, let's hope that a woman driver will one day, very soon, take to a car in a Grand Prix itself and show us what the fairer sex can do when mixing it with the best guys in the world. This has become closer to reality with the news that Williams' development driver Susie Wolff will play a bigger role as test driver with the team after her impressive run in the free practice at the 2014 German Grand Prix when she was only 0.227 seconds slower than Felipe Massa. Her enhanced role will include 2 runs in Free Practice and 2 tests.

So when you have relived the 2014 season with me and hopefully enjoyed the ride, we can take that hat off and throw it into the air and salute this sport that I love above any other and hope that you either love too or that you will grow to love.

THE PROTAGONISTS

Team	Constructor	Chassis	Engine	Drivers
Caterham F1 Team	Caterham Renault	CT05	Renault Energy	Marcus Ericsson Kamui Kobayashi André Lotterer Will Stevens
Scuderia Ferrari	Ferrari	F14 T	Ferrari 059/3	Kimi Räikkönen Fernando Alonso
Sahara Force India F1 Team	Force India Mercedes	VJM07	Mercedes PU106A Hybrid	Sergio Pérez Nico Hulkenberg
Lotus F1 Team	Lotus Renault	E22	Renault Energy F1-2014	Romain Grosjean Pastor Maldonado
Marussia F1 Team	Marussia Ferrari	MR03	Ferrari 059/3	Max Chilton Jules Bianchi
McLaren Mercedes	McLaren Mercedes	MP4-29	Mercedes PU106A Hybrid	Kevin Magnussen Jenson Button
Mercedes AMG Petronas F1 Team	Mercedes	F1 W05 Hybrid	Mercedes PU106A	Nico Rosberg Lewis Hamilton
Infiniti Red Bull Racing	Red Bull Renault	RB10	Renault Energy F1-2014	Sebastian Vettel Daniel Ricciardo
Sauber F1 Team	Sauber Ferrari	C33	Ferrari 059/3	Esteban Gutiérrez Adrian Sutil
Scuderia Toro Rosso	Toro Rosso Renault	STR9	Renault Energy F1-2014	Jean-Eric Vergne Daniil Kvyat
Williams Martini Racing	Williams-Mercedes	FW36	Mercedes PU106A Hybrid	Felipe Massa Valtteri Bottas

THE PROTAGONISTS

44
LEWIS HAMILTON

BORN - 7 JANUARY 1985 (AGE 29)
STEVENAGE, HERTFORDSHIRE, ENGLAND, UK

NATIONALITY - BRITISH
TEAM - MERCEDES
CAR NUMBER - 44
RACES - 129
CHAMPIONSHIPS 1 (2008)
WINS 22
PODIUMS 54
CAREER POINTS 1,102
POLE POSITIONS 31

THE PROTAGONISTS

6
NICO ROSBERG

BORN - 27 JUNE 1985 (AGE 29)
WIESBADEN, HESSE, WEST GERMANY

NATIONALITY - GERMAN
TEAM - MERCEDES
CAR NUMBER - 6
RACES - 147
WINS 3
PODIUMS 11
CAREER POINTS 8570.5
POLE POSITIONS 4

THE PROTAGONISTS

SEBASTIAN VETTEL — 1 — RED BULL

DANIEL RICCIARDO — 3 — RED BULL

FERNANDO ALONSO — 7 — FERRARI

KIMI RAIKKÖNEN — 14 — FERRARI

VALTTERI BOTTAS — 77 — WILLIAMS

FELIPE MASSA — 19 — WILLIAMS

JENSON BUTTON — 22 — MCLAREN

KEVIN MAGNUSSEN — 20 — MCLAREN

NICO HÜLKENBERG — 27 — FORCE INDIA

SERGIO PEREZ — 19 — FORCE INDIA

ROMAIN GROSJEAN — 8 — LOTUS

PASTOR MALDONADO — 13 — LOTUS

THE PROTAGONISTS

25 — JEAN-ÉRIC VERGNE — TORRO ROSSO

26 — DANIIL KVYAT — TORRO ROSSO

99 — ADRIAN SUTIL — SAUBER

ESTEBAN GUTIÉRREZ — 21 — SAUBER

JULES BIANCHI — 17 — MARUSSIA

MAX CHILTON — 4 — MARUSSIA

10 — KAMUI KOBAYASHI — CATERHAM

9 — MARCUS ERICSSON — CATERHAM

ANDRÉ LOTTERER — 45 — CATERHAM

WILL STEVENS — 46 — CATERHAM

CHANGES FOR 2014

In 2014, Formula 1 will hold the Russian Grand Prix, at a street circuit in the Sochi Olympic Park, for the first time. Red Bull reached an agreement with the sport's supremo, Bernie Ecclestone, to revive the Austrian Grand Prix after a 10 year absence from the calendar. The race will be held at the Red Bull Ring, which previously hosted the Austrian Grand Prix in 2003, when the circuit was known as the A1 Ring. The Bahrain Grand Prix will be held at night under lights, similar to the Singapore Grand Prix. The decision to hold the race under lights was taken as a means of marking the 10th anniversary of the event.

The Korean Grand Prix, Mexican Grand Prix, and the Grand Prix of America were included in the provisional calendar first announced in September 2013, but were later removed from the final calendar released in December. The Indian Grand Prix will not be held in 2014 following the devaluation of the Indian Rupee and ongoing complications arising from Indian taxation laws.

2014 TECHNICAL REGULATION CHANGES

The 2014 season has a new engine formula. The new engines are a 1.6 litre V6 with an 8 speed semi-automatic gearbox. The rules require the use of a 90 degree engine bank, with fixed crankshaft and mounting points for the chassis, while the engines are limited to 15,000 rpm. Individual engine units must last for at least 4,000 km (2,500 miles) before being replaced, last year it was 2,000 km (1,200 miles). The engines, now known as power units, are made up of 6 separate components - the internal combustion engine (ICE), turbocharger (TC), the Motor Generator Unit-Kinetic (MGU-K), the Motor Generator Unit-Heat (MGU-H), the Energy Store (ES) and the Control Electronics (CE) unit.

The previous engines used between 2006 to 2013, were subjected to a development 'freeze', which stopped manufacturers from upgrading their engines. With the challenges of the new 2014 engines, the engine freeze was replaced with a points trading system to stop manufacturers from being unable to develop their engines. Under this system, the individual parts of the engine are classified as Tier 1, Tier 2 and Tier 3, and are given a points value each. Engine manufacturers have a budget of 66 points, which can be spent on engine development, with points deducted from their budget depending on the parts developed.

The kinetic energy recovery system, known from 2009 to 2013 as KERS, and renamed from 2014 as ERS-K, is incorporated into the design of the engine. Its function as an extra power source has been taken by the new heat-based energy recovery system (ERS). The ERS unit captures waste heat as it is driven out from the exhaust turbocharger, using an electrical device known as a heat motor generator unit. This waste heat is stored as an electrical charge until it is used by a system called the kinetic motor generator unit. This device is connected to the drive train to deliver the extra power in the most efficient way. In combination with the ERS-K it gives drivers an additional 161 bhp (120 kW) for 33 seconds per lap, compared to the KERS units, which gave drivers 80 bhp (60 kW) for 6 seconds per lap.

Teams were permitted to use electronic braking devices to manage the braking of the rear wheels as the increased power output from the ERS-K units made regulating the brake bias much harder than it had been previously.

Teams may no longer change their gear ratios from race to race to suit the demands of any given circuit. They must nominate eight gear ratios ahead of the first race, and these eight ratios are used all year.

The 2014 regulations required the use of lower noses than in previous years, in the interests of safety. The tip of the nose can be no more than 185 mm (7.3 in) above the ground, in comparison to the 550 mm (22 in) allowed in 2012.

Teams were no longer able to use a beam wing at the rear of the car, a small wing above the diffuser that generates low pressure as air passes over it.

Fuel flow is restricted to 100 kg/h above 10,500 rpm, below 10,500 rpm a formula for the maximum flow must be applied based on the rpm in use.

The position of the exhaust outlet changed so it is now angled upwards toward the rear wing, instead of downwards towards the rear diffuser, so that using exhaust blown diffusers will be difficult.

The minimum weight of the cars was increased from 642 kg (1,415 lb) to 691 kg (1,523 lb) to account for heavier engines, energy recovery units and tyres.

SPORTING REGULATION CHANGES

Mid season testing has returned for 2014, thank goodness. Three European venues each hosted a two-day test in the week following the Grand Prix held at that circuit, with one test after the final round in Abu Dhabi. Teams also had to use one of these days to aid tyre supplier, Pirelli, in the development of their tyres. The end of season Young Driver Tests are discontinued.

The penalty system has been overhauled, with the introduction of a penalty points system for driving offences. With this system, driving offences carry a pre-determined points value based on their severity. These points accrue over the season, with a driver receiving a race ban after accumulating twelve penalty points. Any driver who receives a ban will also get five penalty points when they return, to stop further offences. Penalty points remain on a driver's licence for twelve months.

Stewards were given the power to hand out 5 second penalties in addition to the existing range of penalties within their power. The 5 second penalties were introduced where current penalties are considered too severe. Drivers are permitted to serve these penalties before a regular pit stop, with the driver stopping in their pit bay for 5 seconds before the regular pit-stop begins. The 5 second penalty can also be added to a driver's total race time if they have no pit-stops left.

The rules regarding unsafe pit releases were rewritten, with the driver given a grid penalty for the next race. The pit lane speed limit was reduced from 100 km/h (62 mph) to 80 km/h (50 mph) in the interests of safety.

Drivers are only able to use five engines during the season, down from eight last year. Drivers who use an extra engine start the race from the pit lane. Drivers are only able to use five individual components of their power unit. If a driver goes over this amount for any component, they get a 10 place grid penalty. They would receive an extra 5 place penalty for going over the 5 unit allocation of any other element after the 10 place penalty has been applied.

In the event that a penalty demotes a driver beyond the back row of the grid, the excess penalty is carried over to the next race. They cannot accumulate beyond that.

Drivers can choose their own car numbers between 2 and 99 that they can use throughout their careers. The number 1 is still the World Champion's right.

The FIA have introduced a 'Pole Trophy', awarded to the driver who gets the most pole position in the season. The qualifying time allocation has changed with Q1 being 18 minutes, Q2 is 15 minutes and Q3 is now 12 minutes.

The 107% rule has been changed and will be judged on a case by case basis.

Drivers have to return to the pits under their own power after the chequered flag has fallen.

And, the most controversial of all is that the final race of the season will have double points given to constructors and drivers, in a bid to keep the championship fights alive for longer.

THE PREAMBLE

PRE SEASON TESTING - JEREZ

No one would have believed you if you said that Red Bull would be the team which would struggle the most in the first test in Jerez, after 4 years of dominance and 4 constructors' titles.

Red Bull only completed 21 laps, and they have some serious work to do. Red Bull's Boss, Christian Horner, admitted their problems are "numerous", especially engine cooling. They opened extra vents in the side pods to help, but it failed to do so. The team's press releases are blaming engine supplier, Renault. They did fewer laps than anyone else all week, except for Lotus, who didn't attend. No.2 driver, Daniel Ricciardo admitted it's "back to the drawing board."

Mercedes seem to be the best of the engine manufacturers, with Ferrari behind. The total mileage of the Mercedes' cars shows this. On the Tuesday of the test, Mercedes' powered cars did 36 laps, Ferrari 38, and Renault 19. On Wednesday, Mercedes' powered cars did 212 laps, Ferrari 100, and Renault just 19.

McLaren did better than recent history in Jerez. On track, Button and Magnussen did some good mileage. The team also confirmed the arrival of Eric Boullier, former team principal of Lotus, as racing director. Despite crashing the car on the final day, Magnussen impressed on his debut.

There is no doubt that the new 'power units' are quiet. One the big draws of Formula 1 is the sheer noise. Bernie Ecclestone has criticised the new engines as 'totally absurd'!

PRE-SEASON TESTING - BAHRAIN

Jerez was all about systems checks while the second test in Bahrain focused on performance.

Mercedes and the Mercedes' powered Williams and McLarens teams did around 300 laps over the four days. Red Bull managed a little over 100.

Mercedes are now favourites for victory at next month's Grand Prix in Australia. Nico Rosberg and Lewis Hamilton set the fastest times of the week in Bahrain, and they did 315 laps between them. Rosberg's fastest lap of 1m 33.283s, was under a second off of his 2013 pole position time at the circuit.

After missing Jerez, Lotus had plenty to do as they played catch-up. However, only Marussia did fewer laps.

Red Bull made an improvement in Bahrain. They did 116 laps, fewer than anyone except Lotus and Marussia, and Ricciardo's best lap of 1m 39.837s put them 15th. The team were happy to have resolved the problems of Jerez, but new ones occurred.

While headlines focused on Mercedes' success and Renault's woes, Ferrari were somewhere in-between. Fernando Alonso and Kimi Räikkönendid 287 laps. They finished sixth and seventh in the ranking, although Räikkönencrashed at the end of the test.

Williams were impressive, with Felipe Massa setting the fastest time of the second and final Bahrain sessions.

THE AUSTRALIAN GRAND PRIX

MELBOURNE

ROUND 1
MELBOURNE GRAND PRIX CIRCUIT
AUSTRALIAN GRAND PRIX

MERCEDES IS THE CLASS ACT
DESPITE HAMILTON'S EARLY RETIREMENT

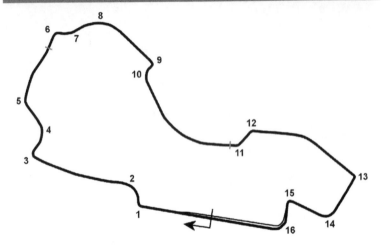

Date: 16 March 2014

Official Name: 2014 Formula 1 Rolex Australian Grand Prix

Circuit: Melbourne Grand Prix Circuit, Albert Park, Melbourne, Australia.
Temporary street circuit

Lap Length: 5.3 km (3.3 miles)

Lap Record: 1m 24.125s - Michael Schumacher (2004)

Race Distance: 58 laps, 307.6 km (191.1 miles)

All talk before the season opener was about the reliability of the new 1.6 litre V6 turbo hybrid engines, with many expecting a decimation of the field through mechanical failures. The new rule changes are such a step up in technology that it seems unlikely that the teams have had enough time or testing to hone their machines into such a state as to last a full race distance. It is the first time since the 1988 Australian Grand Prix, that turbocharged engines have been used in Formula One. That period with the engines didn't turn out to be a qualified success.

With the rule changes regarding the lowering of the noses of the cars, the expected ugly solutions by the teams generally materialised with the ugliest being the distinctive anteater noses, totally out of keeping with the design of the rest of the car. However, Mercedes and Ferrari have come up with solutions that straddle the front wings and are more in keeping with Formula 1's image. McLaren have combined this and the anteater solution.

Tyre supplier Pirelli brought its white-banded medium compound tyre as the harder prime tyre and the yellow-banded soft compound tyre as the softer option tyre.

QUALIFYING

Key (applies to all Grand Prix):

FP1/2/3 - Free Practice 1/2/3, 2 1½ hour sessions on the previous day and 1 1½ session on the morning of Qualification where teams set up the cars for Qualification and the race.

Q1/2/3 - 3 smaller sessions of 18, 15 and 12 minute where teams qualify for the race in the order of fastest times. 6 of the slowest of the 22 cars are eliminated in Q1 and 6 are eliminated in Q2, leaving 10 to shoot it out for the 10 top grid slots.

As qualifying approached, there was the threat of rain, with storms being reported to the west of the circuit, moving east towards the circuit.

In his debut for Red Bull, the likeable Australian, Daniel Ricciardo, set the early pace to the delight of the crowd. After such a great 2013 season, Lotus were really struggling with Pastor Maldonado failing to set a time and Romain Grosjean qualifying a lowly 21st, which became 20th when Sauber's Esteban Gutiérrez was given a penalty for a gearbox change. Max Chilton out-qualified his Marussia team mate Jules Bianchi, but missed out on a place in Q2 by 100th of a second. Caterham driver Marcus Ericsson was the final driver eliminated in Q1, with his team-mate Kamui Kobayashi overcoming a lack of running in all sessions of Free Practice to advance to Q3.

The weather reports proved to be correct as Q2 began. The slippery conditions claimed their first victim in the 2007 World Champion Kimi Räikkönen, who spun his Ferrari late in the session. Räikkönen's spin brought out the yellow flags, meaning drivers had to slow down in that section of the track and several drivers, with the 2009 World Champion Jenson Button and reigning World Champion Sebastian Vettel (World Champion 4 times between 2010 and 2013) both complaining that the incident prevented them from advancing to Q3. Vettel, though, was also hindered by engine problems, which had plagued him since FP3 that morning. Sauber's Adrian Sutil finished the period in 14th, with Kamui Kobayashi 15th after Sergio Pérez spun his Force India on his final flying lap.

The rain was much heavier in the top 10 shootout, with several drivers venturing out on full wet tyres. The race for the pole became a 3 way fight between the Mercedes drivers, 2008 World Champion Lewis Hamilton, Nico Rosberg and Red Bull's Daniel Ricciardo, on his debut for the team. It eventually came down to the final runs in Q3 where Hamilton set the fastest time, Ricciardo qualifying a career-best 2nd in his home race, and Rosberg, who was 3rd. A delighted Kevin Magnussen, in his rookie year, qualified his McLaren in 4th. After Räikkönen's Q2 spin had left him 12th, with 2 times World Champion (2005 and 2006) Fernando Alonso giving Ferrari a decent result when he recovered to 5th after making the wrong tyre choice early in the period and started next to the Toro Rosso of Jean-Éric Vergne. Force India's Nico Hülkenberg and debutant Daniil Kvyat filled the next row of the grid, ahead of the Williams pair of Felipe Massa and Valtteri Bottas, who, like Gutierrez, was demoted 5 places for a gearbox change. For Williams, it was the first time since the 2012 Hungarian Grand Prix that both cars made it into Q3.

QUALIFYING RESULT (Top 10)

Q3	Car No.	Driver (Constructor)	Q1 Time	Q2 Time	Q3 Time	Grid Pos.
1	44	**Lewis Hamilton** **Mercedes**	**1:31.699**	**1:42.890**	**1:44.231**	1
2	3	Daniel Ricciardo Red Bull	1:30.775	1:42.295	1:44.548	2
3	6	Nico Rosberg Mercedes	1:32.564	1:42.264	1:44.595	3
4	20	Kevin Magnussen McLaren	1:30.949	1:43.247	1:45.745	4
5	14	Fernando Alonso Ferrari	1:31.388	1:42.805	1:45.819	5
6	25	Jean-Eric Vergne Toro Rosso	1:33.488	1:43.849	1:45.864	6
7	27	Nico Hülkenberg Force India	1:33.893	1:43.658	1:46.030	7
8	26	Daniil Kvyat Toro Rosso	1:33.777	1:44.331	1:47.368	8
9	19	Felipe Massa Williams	1:31.228	1:44.242	1:48.079	9
10	77	Valtteri Bottas Williams	1:31.601	1:43.852	1:48.147	15

Valtteri Bottas - five-place grid penalty for changing a gearbox.

Max Chilton, Jules Bianchi and Romain Grosjean started the race from pit lane. Esteban Gutiérrez - five-place grid penalty for changing a gearbox.

Pastor Maldonado failed to set a lap time within 107% of the fastest lap time set by Daniel Ricciardo in Q1. Later, he was given permission to start by race stewards.

THE RACE

As the lights went out on the first race of the season, both Marussia drivers Max Chilton and Jules Bianchi were left behind, after both suffered problems during the formation lap. Lotus' Romain Grosjean started the race from the pit lane after having modifications made to his car in Parc Fermé (only a limited number of changes are allowed under these conditions) and compounded this when he was given a drive-through penalty for leaving his pit garage before the 15 minute mark prior to the race.

Nico Rosberg made the better start of the front runners, coming from behind in third to take the lead at the first corner. Lewis Hamilton had a sluggish start from the pole position and seemed to be immediately struggling and was down to 4th behind Rosberg and Ricciardo by the first corner. Over the ensuing corners he struggled to maintain his position and was down to 5th by the end of the first lap and was called into the pits by his team a short while later, on lap 3. It later transpired that Hamilton had had a cylinder failure from the very start of the race.

Meanwhile, shortly after the start of the race, Williams' Felipe Massa, Caterham's Kamui Kobayashi and Ferrari's Kimi Räikkönen were involved in a collision, putting Kobayashi and Massa out of the race whilst Räikkönen's Ferrari was able to continue without further problems although he had minor damage. Kobayashi had suffered a loss of rear brakes and it was the first of many DNFs (Did Not Finish) for Felipe Massa, through no fault of his own. The reigning World Champion, Sebastian Vettel, was also hit by engine trouble in his Red Bull, retiring a lap later than Hamilton.

With Mercedes clearly the class act of the field, Hamilton's early retirement left Rosberg unopposed out front and the German drove a controlled race to lead until the end, comfortably beating home favourite Daniel Ricciardo by some 24 seconds.

It was the German's 4th career win, and he was clearly overjoyed at the car's performance. "It's been an amazing day," said Rosberg. "I'm over the moon really, everyone has worked so hard over the winter and to have such an amazing Silver Arrow. I'm really thankful to Mercedes for giving me such an amazing car. There is a lot of work still to do. We can still improve a lot and we must because the competitors are not going to be asleep."

Daniel Ricciardo's 2nd place finish made him the first Australian Formula One driver to finish on the podium in his home race when it has been a World Championship points scoring race.

Surprisingly, it was also the first time that Red Bull had completed the equivalent of a race distance since it first took to the track at the end of January (the team had previously not managed to do more than 20 laps in a row in pre-season testing). The Australian was in a comfortable 2nd for most of the race but came under significant pressure from Magnussen in the final 20 laps, who closed the gap to within a second, and in the DRS zone with 5 laps to go, (DRS - Drag Reduction Zone: There are up to 2 zones situated on the straights at all Grand Prix, where a driver can open the slots in the rear wing, which reduces drag and gains you 12-15km/hour in straight line speed. It is only activated if the pursuing car is within 1 second of the car ahead at the activation point and is only enabled after 2 laps of the race. It is un-enabled under safety car conditions or any other extenuating circumstances at the discretion of the race official, Charlie Whiting) but finally maintained the gap till the end to mark an impressive debut for the Red Bull team, "Two or three weeks ago I would have bet pretty much everything I had that we would not be standing up there," Ricciardo said.

McLaren showed early promise, as Danish rookie Kevin Magnussen finished 3rd, only 2 seconds behind Ricciardo. This made him the first Formula One debutant since Lewis Hamilton at the 2007 Australian Grand Prix seven years earlier to finish on the podium and the first podium finish in a World Championship Grand Prix by a Danish driver.

Fourth was Magnussen's team mate Jenson Button, finishing 4 seconds behind his inexperienced team mate and unable to close the gap on him - although he beat Alonso, who finished 5th, by jumping ahead of the Ferrari at their final pit stops. Then Valtteri Bottas followed in 6th (despite the Williams' driver flirting with one of the infamous Melbourne walls on the exit of Turn 10 while running 5th and causing a puncture to his right rear tyre on lap 11 thus triggering the safety car.) The Finn dropped back to 16th place but used the pace of the Williams to fight back up through the field.

Force India's Nico Hülkenberg finished 7th, after running 4th in the early stages when he jumped up from 7th on the grid and passed Alonso on the first lap. Despite winning last year in a Lotus, now a Ferrari driver, Kimi Räikkönen finished a disappointing 8th. Jean-Éric Vergne was in 9th and the impressive Russian rookie, Daniil Kvyat in 10th, thus becoming the youngest ever points scorer in Formula One, at the age of 19, thus taking the honour away from Sebastian Vettel!

According to the team, both Ferraris suffered electrical problems during the race.

With Vettel retiring, it was the first time since the 2013 Hungarian Grand Prix that Vettel had failed to win, after 9 wins in a row to run away with the 2013 World Championship. Unreliability, although not as bad as the doomsayers were predicting, was still a worrying factor as 8 cars failed to finish as Formula 1 began its new era of high-tech turbo hybrid engines and a limit of no more than 100kg of fuel for a race distance (measured in weight rather than volume as volume can change during a race due to the temperature variations, while weight remains a constant).

POST RACE

Despite retiring so early from the race, Mercedes' Lewis Hamilton was surprisingly upbeat about his season going forward although this may have something to do with the dominance that the sister car had for the rest of the race and gives him hope that next time out it will be his turn. "My start didn't feel great today and I had a lot less power than usual when pulling away," he said, "so it was obvious immediately that something was wrong. It looks like we only had five cylinders firing and, while I wanted to keep going, we had to play safe and save the engine. It's unfortunate but that's racing and we will recover from this. We have a great car and engine, and the pace was really strong today as Nico clearly showed."

Disappointment ensued for Daniel Ricciardo and Red Bull when they were disqualified around six hours after the end of the race for a fuel-flow rate infringement. He was excluded from the race result for a breach of Article 5.1.4 of the Formula One Technical Regulations, which govern the maximum allowable rate at which fuel may flow into the engine. The team were also referred to the stewards for using an unauthorised method of measuring the fuel flow. However, the team immediately announced their intention to appeal the Stewards' decision claiming that the sensors provided by the FIA to measure the Fuel flow are unreliable. The appeal was heard by the FIA on 14 April, but it was rejected and the disqualification was upheld. The decision promoted the Dane, Kevin

Magnussen, who drove magnificently for McLaren on his debut, to 2nd. "It's hard to believe," said Magnussen. "It seems so surreal. The car was so much better than it has been at any point. I just had exactly what I needed the whole race. The preparation we have done this winter has been fantastic."

Kamui Kobayashi was referred to the stewards as well for his involvement in the first-lap collision with Felipe Massa and Kimi Räikkönen. The stewards decided not to take any further action against the Japanese driver after they determined the accident was triggered by a mechanical failure on Kobayashi's Caterham.

AUSTRALIAN GRAND PRIX 2014 RACE RESULT

Pos.	No.	Driver (Constructor)	Laps	Time	Grid	Points
1	6	**Nico Rosberg Mercedes**	57	1:32:58.710	3	25
2	20	Kevin Magnussen McLaren-Mercedes	57	+26.777	4	18
3	22	Jenson Button McLaren-Mercedes	57	+30.027	10	15
4	14	Fernando Alonso Ferrari	57	+35.284	5	12
5	77	Valtteri Bottas Williams-Mercedes	57	+47.639	15	10
6	27	Nico Hülkenberg Force India-Mercedes	57	+50.718	7	8
7	7	Kimi Räikkönen Ferrari	57	+57.675	11	6
8	25	Jean-Eric Vergne Toro Rosso-Renault	57	+1:00.441	6	4
9	26	Daniil Kvyat Toro Rosso-Renault	57	+1:03.585	8	2
10	11	Sergio Pérez Force India-Mercedes	57	+1:25.916	16	1

Jules Bianchi - did not complete 90% of the race distance, and therefore was not classified as a finisher.

Daniel Ricciardo - disqualified for breaching the maximum fuel limit and using an unauthorised method of measuring fuel consumption.

DRIVERS' CHAMPIONSHIP

Pos.	Driver	Points
1	**Nico Rosberg**	**25**
2	Kevin Magnussen	18
3	Jenson Button	15
4	Fernando Alonso	12
5	Valtteri Bottas	10

CONSTRUCTORS' CHAMPIONSHIP

Pos.	Constructor	Points
1	**McLaren-Mercedes**	**33**
2	Mercedes	25
3	Ferrari	18
4	Williams-Mercedes	10
5	Force India-Mercedes	9

THE MALAYSIAN GRAND PRIX

SEPANG

ROUND 2
SEPANG INTERNATIONAL CIRCUIT
MALAYSIAN GRAND PRIX

HAMILTON CLOSES GAP ON ROSBERG

MERCEDES STAMP THEIR AUTHORITY

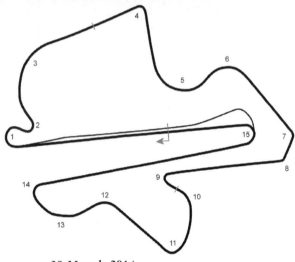

Date: 30 March 2014

Official Name: 2014 Formula 1 Petronas Malaysia Grand Prix

Circuit: Sepang International Circuit, Sepang, Selangor, Malaysia

Lap Length: 5.5 km (3.4 miles)

Lap Record: 1m 34.223s - Juan Pablo Montoya (2004)

Distance: 56 laps, 310.4 km (192.8 miles)

Pirelli again brought the same tyres as for last year's Malaysian Grand Prix, the orange-banded hard compound tyre as the harder prime tyre and the white-banded medium compound tyre as the softer option tyre.

Prior to the race, there was a minute's silence as a mark of respect to the passengers of Malaysia Airlines Flight 370, which disappeared over the Indian Ocean three weeks prior to the race. The drivers also carried messages on their cars and on their helmets.

QUALIFYING

The start of Q1 was delayed for 50 minutes due to torrential rain. The track had now dried out enough for intermediate tyres to be used although McLaren chose to go out on extreme wet tyres. More rain was predicted, so the drivers had to go out early in order to get some quick times while the rain held off. Mercedes' team mates Nico Rosberg and Lewis Hamilton lined up at the pit exit to be the first out.

With 11 minutes remaining of the 18 minute session Rosberg led Hamilton by 200th of a second and the rain was getting heavier on some sections of the circuit. Daniel Ricciardo was in third place while his Red Bull teammate was struggling with Sebastian Vettel in 10th. With only 4 minutes remaining in the session, Vettel managed to get to third and then slid off at Turn 9 in the treacherous conditions. The 6 drivers eliminated at the end of Q1 were Pastor Maldonado, Adrian Sutil, Jules Bianchi, Kamui Kobayashi, Max Chilton and Marcus Ericsson.

During the small break between Q1 and Q2 the rain began to fall heavier, but was not enough to cause any more delays. But the track was now much wetter and Hamilton and Rosberg went out on extreme wets. The other drivers followed suit except for Alonso, Räikkönen and Bottas, who gambled with intermediates.

Again everybody was on track to try and set a fast time before the weather closed in. However, Alonso, possibly due to his gamble with the tyres, clipped Daniel Kvyat's Toro Rosso, and the red flags stopped the session after just two minutes. The Ferrari's left front suspension was damaged.

Q2 resumed after 6 minutes and everyone went out on extremes except for Bottas. Hamilton set the mark with Bottas on intermediates some 10 seconds off of his pace. With only 2 minutes remaining in the session, Hamilton improved on his previous time while Rosberg moved up to second. Then at the least minute Vettel snatched second in the ever improving Red Bull although in the dry they may have been struggling.

The top 6 at the end of Q2 were: Hamilton, Vettel, Rosberg, Ricciardo, Hulkenberg and Alonso. The 6 drivers eliminated at the end of Q2 were: Kvyat, Gutierrez, Massa, Pérez, Bottas and Grosjean.

For Q3 the question was what tyres were right at this time. Most drivers opted for the extremes, except the McLarens who made the wrong choice and again had to swap, losing valuable track time.

Hamilton set a fast time of 1m 59.431s, considering the conditions. With only 4 minutes remaining in the session, the track was starting to dry off but it wasn't enough for a switch to inters. On their final laps, Vettel moved into 2nd, Alonso was 3rd, Rosberg 4th and Ricciardo 5th. On his final fast run Hamilton ran wide at Turn 4 and continued but couldn't improve. Just as the chequered flag came out, Rosberg, on his final lap, snatched third from Alonso while everyone else failed to improve.

The top 10 qualifiers at the end of Q3 were: Hamilton, Vettel, Rosberg, Alonso, Ricciardo, Räikkönen Hulkenberg, Magnussen, Jean-Éric Vergne (Toro Rosso) and Button who had stayed out on inters for the entire session.

QUALIFYING RESULT (Top 10)

Q3	Car No.	Driver (Constructor)	Q1 Time	Q2 Time	Q3 Time	Grid Pos.
1	44	**Lewis Hamilton** **Mercedes**	**1:57.202**	**1:59.041**	**1:59.431**	1
2	1	Sebastian Vettel Red Bull	1:57.654	1:59.399	1:59.486	2
3	6	Nico Rosberg Mercedes	1:57.183	1:59.445	2:00.050	3
4	14	Fernando Alonso Ferrari	1:58.889	2:01.356	2:00.175	4
5	3	Daniel Ricciardo Red Bull	1:58.913	2:00.147	2:00.541	5
6	7	Kimi Räikkönen Ferrari	1:59.257	2:01.532	2:01.218	6
7	27	Nico Hülkenberg Force India	1:58.883	2:00.839	2:01.712	7
8	20	Kevin Magnussen McLaren	2:00.356	2:02.094	2:02.213	8
9	25	Jean-Eric Vergne Toro Rosso	2:01.689	2:02.096	2:03.078	9
10	22	Jenson Button McLaren	2:00.889	2:01.810	2:04.053	10

Valtteri Bottas - 3 place grid penalty for impeding Daniel Ricciardo during qualifying.

THE RACE

Lights out and Lewis Hamilton makes a great getaway from the line. Rosberg jumped Sebastian Vettel from 3rd on the grid to 2nd in the first corner. He held on to the spot for the rest of the race with the exception of three laps when Nico Hülkenberg, who was on a two stop strategy whereas - almost everybody else pitted three times - took over the position in his Force India. Hulkenberg had also had a good start from 7th place before getting stuck behind Fernando Alonso. Gearbox problems for Sergio Pérez meant he could not start the race.

There was a first lap incident when Pastor Maldonado and Jules Bianchi collided with one another, effectively ending the race for both of them when they subsequently had mechanical complications due to the incident. (Bianchi later received a penalty for his part in the collision.) At the end of the first lap, the top four were Hamilton, Rosberg, Vettel and Ricciardo - who were now breaking away from the rest of the pack and this sequence remained unchanged until the last 10 laps of the race.

Räikkönen's miserable start to his Ferrari career part 2 continued when Kevin Magnussen's McLaren clipped his right rear tyre going into the first corner on lap 2, causing him a puncture and he eventually finished a lowly 12th.

Hulkenberg fought bravely with Alonso for 4th, but ultimately lost it due to Alonso's fresher tyres, as Force India gambled on a 2 stop pit strategy, while others in the top 5 stuck to three stops. The Williams' duo of Massa and Bottas and McLaren's Button battled for 6th place. It was during this battle that Felipe Massa was sharply reminded of the instruction from Rob Smedley to let Alonso through, made some years earlier, when he was the Ferrari No.2 and when team orders were banned. This time it was Bottas who was intended to be the beneficiary when Massa was told, "Felipe, Valtteri is faster than you." Massa chose not to hear the instruction.

Both Saubers of Adrian Sutil and Esteban Gutiérrez had to retire due to an electrical failure and a gearbox failure respectively. Ricciardo again was having another solid race and looking good for 4th until his 3rd pit stop, when the team released him before his left-front tyre was securely engaged. He was pushed back into the pits but later his front wing failed and he had to retire. After 2 excellent races for his new team - where he has easily proved to be a match for his new 4 time World Champion team mate, Sebastian Vettel - he has, through no fault of his own, ended up with no points on the board. After the race he said, "It was looking like we could have a solid points finish today. The race was going pretty well. The start was really good and I made up a couple of positions and I was starting to, let's say, mix it up at the front, which is nice. It's fun being up there and fighting for the top few spot. But then we had a problem at the last pit stop and then we had a puncture. I think we had a front wing failure and a few other things went on and then the stop-go penalty, so the race ended pretty quickly for us, it went from looking good to looking pretty bad in a short amount of time." Ricciardo, with his beaming smile and friendly demeanour has certainly been a welcome part of the paddock and is now showing some of the promise that Red Bull have seen in him.

The Mercedes' team again showed that they really have a handle on the rule changes for 2014 as Hamilton led every lap of the race, set the fastest lap and therefore achieved his first Grand Chelem of his career. Rosberg's solid 2nd place gives Mercedes their first 1-2 finish since the 1955 Italian Grand Prix. Vettel finished 3rd and giving hope to Red Bull that their pre-season testing disasters are a thing of the past. Alonso came in fourth after a last-lap battle with Hulkenberg who finished fifth, almost 40 seconds ahead of McLaren's Jenson Button, who eventually was able to hold off both Massa and Bottas. Magnussen was 9th for McLaren and the top ten was rounded off by Daniil Kvyat who for the second race in a row finishes in the points.

Lewis Hamilton was extremely excited after the race, not just for himself but for the Mercedes' historic 1-2 finish. "It's my eighth year here and finally I got that win. I really just owe it all to the team. They did a fantastic job, the guys back at the factory pushing non-stop to get the car to where it is, and of course to do it for (fuel partner) Petronas on our home ground almost, to get a one-two, I mean it's quite special when you get a one-two. I've not had many in my career and so that makes it even more special. I'm really grateful for all the work that's done. A great day."

Rosberg, who still leads the championship said, "I had a great start again, even though it was tight with Sebastian. It was very close at the wall and I just closed my eyes, went for the gap and did it. Later I was able to control the pace and to defend my position against Seb but Lewis was out of my reach, so congratulations to him for his win."

Behind them Sebastian Vettel was pleased with the progress of his Red Bull. "I thought I had a good start, but then I focused on getting in the tow of Lewis to maybe attack him going into the first corner. Then Nico was there on the right and it was quite tight. Daniel was coming as well as I was trying to get past Nico. So I lost a place but fortunately I got it back and then later on I was trying to get as close as I could to Nico. At some stage it looked like we are pretty similar, pretty evenly matched but then it's like he found another gear, he was pulling away."

"We need to make big steps because they are quite far ahead," Vettel continued, "but I'm quite happy with the steps we're currently making. It's the first race distance I've done this year, since Brazil, it's the first race distance I've done so that's a big step. Obviously, at some stage during testing, we didn't expect to finish the first couple of races so well done to all the guys in the team on the reliability front. It's not a big secret, we know there's still a lot to do. In terms of drivability we're not yet there where we want to be. In terms of power, it's not a big secret without giving a hammering but the guys at Viry are flat out to work on that front. Renault is pushing very, very hard but at this stage we have to summarize and say that Mercedes did a better job, they're quicker than us so we know that there are a lot of things we have to do better but it's still a bloody good result today, finishing on the podium."

POST RACE

Daniel Ricciardo was given a 10 place grid penalty for the next Grand Prix after the Red Bull team released his car in an unsafe manner from his pit box. Kevin Magnussen and Jules Bianchi also received two penalty points each, along with Valtteri Bottas after Bottas was accused of impeding Ricciardo during qualifying.

MALAYSIAN GRAND PRIX 2014 RACE RESULT

Pos.	No.	Driver (Constructor)	Laps	Time	Grid	Points
1	**44**	**Lewis Hamilton** **Mercedes**	**56**	**1:40:25.974**	**1**	**25**
2	6	Nico Rosberg Mercedes	56	+17.313	3	18
3	1	Sebastian Vettel Red Bull-Renault	56	+24.534	2	15
4	14	Fernando Alonso Ferrari	56	+35.992	4	12
5	27	Nico Hülkenberg Force India-Mercedes	56	+47.199	7	10
6	22	Jenson Button McLaren-Mercedes	56	+1:23.691	10	8
7	19	Felipe Massa Williams-Mercedes	56	+1:25.076	13	6
8	77	Valtteri Bottas Williams-Mercedes	56	+1:25.537	18	4
9	20	Kevin Magnussen McLaren-Mercedes	55	+1 Lap	8	2
10	26	Daniil Kvyat Toro Rosso-Renault	55	+1 Lap	11	1

DRIVERS' CHAMPIONSHIP

Pos.	Driver	Points
1	**Nico Rosberg**	**43**
2	Lewis Hamilton	25
3	Fernando Alonso	24
4	Jenson Button	23
5	Kevin Magnussen	20

CONSTRUCTORS' CHAMPIONSHIP

Pos.	Constructor	Points
1	**Mercedes**	**68**
2	McLaren-Mercedes	43
3	Ferrari	30
4	Williams-Mercedes	20
5	Force India-Mercedes	19

THE BAHRAIN GRAND PRIX

SAKHIR

ROUND 3
BAHRAIN INTERNATIONAL CIRCUIT
BAHRAIN GRAND PRIX

HAMILTON'S SLAP ACROSS THE BOWS
FIRST CLOSE ENCOUNTER
HAMILTON 1 ROSBERG 0

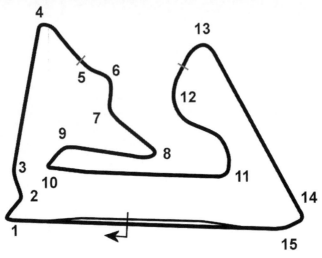

Date: 6 April 2014

Official Name: 2014 Formula 1 Gulf Air Bahrain Grand Prix

Circuit: Bahrain International Circuit, Sakhir, Bahrain

Lap Length: 5.4 km (3.4 miles)

Lap Record: 1m 31.447s – Pedro De La Rosa (2005)

Distance: 57 laps, 308.2 km (191.5 miles)

THE RETURN OF THE SILVER ARROWS

The 2014 Bahrain Grand Prix, marked the 10th time that the Bahrain Grand Prix had been held as a round of the Formula One World Championship and the 900th World Championship event. Like the Singapore Grand Prix (to be held later in the year) the race was held at night for the first time. The decision to hold the race under lights was taken as a means of marking the tenth anniversary of the event.

Tyre supplier Pirelli brought its white-banded medium compound tyre as the harder prime tyre and the yellow-banded soft compound tyre as the softer option tyre, as opposed to the previous year where hard and medium selections were provided.

QUALIFYING

Again the Mercedes appear to be unstoppable as qualifying approached. Lewis Hamilton had been quickest in all three Free Practice sessions for the Bahrain Grand Prix. In Q1 Daniel Ricciardo continued his upward curve in the Red Bull team, with the fastest time early on. The Mercedes' boys came out for one run and topped the time sheets, 8 minutes into the session, on the medium slower tyres and sat the rest of the session out to save their faster softer tyres for later in qualifying. Bottas grabs P1 with a 1m 34.394s lap time, but Hulkenberg beats that with a 1m 34.934s. Hamilton and Rosberg, safe from elimination and unperturbed by not topping the session, were sat in their respective pit garages, the only ones not on the track.

Q1 top 6 were Hulkenberg, Bottas, Pérez, Massa, Räikkönen and Alonso while the 6 drivers eliminated at the end of Q1 were Maldonado, Sutil, Kobayashi, Bianchi, Ericsson and Chilton.

In Q2 everyone went onto the softer tyre, except for the 2 Williams' who were gambling with the medium tyres. With 9 minutes remaining, Hulkenberg recorded the fastest time of 1m 35.682s, but was immediately eclipsed by Räikkönen with a 1m 34.925s and then again by Hamilton with a 1m 33.872s. 2 minutes later Rosberg took P1 (top spot) with a 1m 33.708s while Daniel Ricciardo was 3rd in his Red Bull with a 1m 34.592s. Vettel left it late to do his first run and with only 1 minute remaining in the session, he could only set a time that gave him 9th. Massa, now on softs, slotted into 8th, but subsequently Vettel was pushed down to 11th and so missed the cut for Q3.

Q2 top 10 were Rosberg, Hamilton, Ricciardo, Button, Alonso, Pérez, Bottas, Massa, Kevin Magnussen and Räikkönen. The 6 drivers eliminated from Q3 were Vettel, Hulkenberg, Kvyat, Vergne, Gutierrez and Grosjean.

Wherever Ricciardo ended up in Q3, he would lose 10 grid places as his penalty for the team giving him an unsafe release from the pit box in Malaysia.

In Q3 with 6 minutes remaining, Rosberg struck first with a 1m 33.185s while Hamilton was second with a 1m 33.464s. 5 minutes later and with everybody on track, the top five were Rosberg, Hamilton, Bottas, Pérez and Massa. However, on his final run, Hamilton went off the track and Rosberg was guaranteed pole position whatever time he set in his last lap. Ricciardo leaped to 3rd and Bottas was 4th.

QUALIFYING RESULT (Top 10)

Q3	Car No.	Driver (Constructor)	Q1 Time	Q2 Time	Q3 Time	Grid Pos.
1	6	**Nico Rosberg** Mercedes	**1:35.439**	**1:33.708**	**1:33.185**	1
2	44	Lewis Hamilton Mercedes	1:35.323	1:33.872	1:33.464	2
3	3	Daniel Ricciardo Red Bull	1:36.220	1:34.592	1:34.051	13
4	77	Valtteri Bottas Williams	1:34.934	1:34.842	1:34.247	3
5	11	Sergio Pérez Force India	1:34.998	1:34.747	1:34.346	4
6	7	Kimi Räikkönen Ferrari	1:35.234	1:34.925	1:34.368	5
7	22	Jenson Button McLaren	1:35.699	1:34.714	1:34.387	6
8	19	Felipe Massa Williams	1:35.085	1:34.842	1:34.511	7
9	20	Kevin Magnussen McLaren	1:35.288	1:34.904	1:34.712	8
10	14	Fernando Alonso Ferrari	1:35.251	1:34.723	1:34.992	9

Daniel Ricciardo - 10 place grid penalty for an unsafe pit release during the Malaysian Grand Prix.

Adrian Sutil - 5 place grid penalty for impeding Romain Grosjean during qualifying.

THE RACE

It seems that for now, with the Mercedes engine/aero package being so far out in front of all other challengers, the only challenge that was left, was that between these 2 drivers, these 2 old friends, these 2 immensely competitive individuals. Last year all had been harmonious at Mercedes between the two who had started their friendly but competitive rivalry in their Karting days as aspiring 12 year olds and team mates. Then their dreams came true, firstly for Nico as a Williams' driver at this very Grand Prix in 2006 and a year later for Lewis as a driver for McLaren who had been nurturing him since, aged 10, he famously approached McLaren boss Ron Dennis for an autograph, and told him, "Hi. I'm Lewis Hamilton. I won the British Championship and one day I want to be racing your cars." Dennis wrote in his autograph book, "Phone me in nine years, we'll sort something out then." (Ron Dennis actually called him in 1998, after Hamilton had won a Super One series and his second British Championship, and honouring his promise, signed Hamilton to the McLaren driver development program. The contract included an option to drive for Formula 1, which would eventually make Hamilton the youngest ever driver to secure a contract which later resulted in a Formula 1 drive).

Now, their ultimate dream of being team mates in a potentially championship winning car in Formula 1 had come to fruition. The 2014 Bahrain Grand Prix was to take their intense competitiveness up one notch as they began to realise that their biggest rival, for a now potential drivers' championship, was most probably going to be their team mate. This was the race when the championship really began and the racing became not only more intense, but also more exciting. Prior to the race Ferrari president Luca Di Montezemolo had criticised the new efficiency based Formula 1 for being like 'taxi driving'. But those observations were made to look a little ridiculous by the thrilling Grand Prix that followed, featuring breathless action from start to finish throughout the entire field.

Again, Lewis made a better start as the 5 red lights went out and he took the lead at the first corner. Massa made a great start which launched him to 3rd from 7th, Pérez in 4th, Bottas falls back to 5th, Button 6th, followed by Alonso, Hulkenberg, Räikkönen, Vettel and Magnussen. Jean-Éric Vergne spins and damages his rear end. On lap 4 Hamilton sets another fast lap at 1m 40.5s and leads Rosberg by 1.2 seconds and Hulkenberg passes Alonso into the Turn 1 to take 7th place, with Alonso complaining, on the radio, of not having enough power. The top seven runners are all powered by the all conquering Mercedes' engines.

On lap 7 Mercedes radio Hamilton and tell him to look after his front tyres. Rosberg stayed close to him in these early stages, within 1½ seconds, as they approached their first set of pit stops. Lap 16 and Vettel is told that his team mate is quicker, and to let him by, although Vettel is suffering with no DRS.

Then on lap 18 there occurred the first of many close encounters between the 2. The German dived for the inside at the start of the lap and for a brief moment was past Hamilton, only to run wide and see his team mate chop back across his nose to reclaim the lead. It was a real slap in the face for Rosberg - aggressive driving from Lewis, yes - but completely fair. Rosberg said to his engineer over the radio to, "Warn him that was not on."

He tried again the following lap, but again Hamilton held him off, this time by edging him wide as Rosberg attempted to go around the outside of Turn 4. The two Mercedes' team mates continued to battle closely till Hamilton pits on lap 20 for softs and Rosberg is told to put his foot down until he pits 2 laps later and puts on the medium tyre. Now on different tyre strategies, Hamilton begins to eke out a bigger lead and by lap 40 Hamilton leads Rosberg by 9.5 seconds, followed by Pérez (47.2s further behind), Hulkenberg (2.1s), Bottas (0.2s), Alonso (4.1s), Button (0.4s), Vettel (9.5s), Ricciardo (1.6s) and Massa (1.1s).

Lap 41 and Hamilton's significant lead is wiped out when Gutierrez is smashed in the side while entering Turn 1 by Maldonado, who was coming out of the pits. The Sauber is launched into a flip and barrel rolls, but the Mexican driver is quickly out of the car and the safety car is deployed. Maldonado was handed a 10 second stop/go penalty during the race, but the stewards decided to give him a further 5 place grid penalty for the next race in China and added three points to his super-licence, for the same incident. Gutierrez said of the incident, "First of all, the most important thing is that I am ok. They did all the checks at the hospital and everything is fine. Concerning the accident, I was completely surprised that Pastor, who came out of the pits, ran into me. I was clearly in front of him. I turned into the corner and I was suddenly hit and I rolled over. There was nothing much I could do." While Maldonado seemed to put the onus more on the Mexican, "We will need to have a look again at what happened as Esteban seemed to be off his line coming into turn one - maybe he missed his braking point, I don't know - and by then I was in the corner with nowhere to go. For sure it's difficult to understand and I was coming out from the pits and with cold tyres. I think he was very unlucky and it's good he jumped straight out of the car."

What is true, though, is that the safety car presented us with a fascinating last stint duel, between the 2 Mercedes' cars because after their 2nd pit stops, Hamilton found himself on the slower, medium tyres, while Rosberg was now close behind on the faster, softer tyres.

On lap 52 Rosberg gets ever closer to the back of Hamilton's car. The two Mercedes are side by side and Rosberg takes the lead but Hamilton gets back in front as they go wheel to wheel. Exciting stuff and Hamilton is absolutely determined to keep ahead of his team mate. The next lap and Rosberg again dives down the inside of Hamilton in Turn 1 under DRS. Hamilton crosses back over and grabs back the lead. He tried again the following lap, but again Hamilton held him off, this time by edging him wide as Rosberg attempted to go around the outside of Turn 4. Mercedes were certainly true to their word when they said they would let their drivers race for victory untroubled by team orders.

With four laps to go, the grip was dropping off on Rosberg's tyres, exacerbated by following in the dirty air of the sister car ahead, which degrades the tyres quicker than if they were running in clean air. Hamilton thus began to build a bit of a margin, of about a second and was able to win his second Grand Prix victory of the season and close the gap to Rosberg in the drivers' championship to 11 points. "Nico drove fantastically well throughout, very fair," said Hamilton. "He was very fast on the option tyres at the end. I was on a knife edge throughout, but it was great fun."

"I strongly dislike finishing second to Lewis but on the other hand it was the most exciting race I have ever had in my whole career," said Rosberg. "Today was a day for the sport. I hope you all had a lot of fun. The team played it as fair as they possibly could today. Let us race flat out. I don't think you need any more evidence that we are here to race and there are no team orders."

The racing was just as thrilling behind as Pérez beat Ricciardo by just 0.4 seconds and, 4 seconds behind them, Hulkenberg held off a train of cars running nose to tail all the way down to Räikkönen in 10th. A great race that should lay to bed any criticisms that there is no racing in the new Formula 1.

BAHRAIN GRAND PRIX 2014 RACE RESULT

Pos.	No.	Driver (Constructor)	Laps	Time	Grid	Points
1	44	**Lewis Hamilton** **Mercedes**	**57**	**1:39:42.743**	**2**	**25**
2	6	Nico Rosberg Mercedes	57	+1.085	1	18
3	11	Sergio Pérez Force India-Mercedes	57	+24.067	4	15
4	3	Daniel Ricciardo Red Bull-Renault	57	+24.489	13	12
5	27	Nico Hülkenberg Force India-Mercedes	57	+28.654	11	10
6	1	Sebastian Vettel Red Bull-Renault	57	+29.879	10	8
7	19	Felipe Massa Williams-Mercedes	57	+31.265	7	6
8	77	Valtteri Bottas Williams-Mercedes	57	+31.876	3	4
9	14	Fernando Alonso Ferrari	57	+32.595	9	2
10	7	Kimi Räikkönen Ferrari	57	+33.462	5	1

DRIVERS' CHAMPIONSHIP

Pos. Driver Points

1	**Nico Rosberg**	**61**
2	Lewis Hamilton	50
3	Nico Hülkenberg	28
4	Fernando Alonso	26
5	Jenson Button	23

CONSTRUCTORS' CHAMPIONSHIP

Pos.	Constructor	Points
1	**Mercedes**	111
2	Force India-Mercedes	44
3	McLaren-Mercedes	43
4	Red Bull-Renault	35
5	Ferrari	33

THE CHINESE GRAND PRIX

SHANGHAI

ROUND 4
SHANGHAI INTERNATIONAL CIRCUIT
CHINESE GRAND PRIX

LEWIS WRITES HIS FIRST TRILOGY
MERCEDES REINFORCE THEIR HEGEMONY

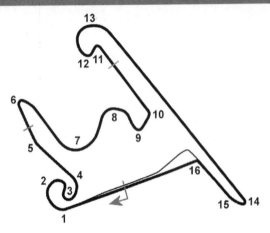

Date: 20 April 2014

Official Name: 2014 Formula 1 UBS Chinese Grand Prix

Circuit: Shanghai International Circuit, Shanghai, People's Republic of China

Lap Length: 5.5 km (3.4 miles)

Lap Record: 1m 32.238s - Michael Schumacher (2004)

Distance: 54 laps, 294.2 km (182.8 miles)

Scheduled Distance: 56 laps, 305 km (189.6 miles)

So, Nico Rosberg was leading the Drivers' Championship with 61 points with Lewis Hamilton now only 11 points behind Rosberg. Behind Rosberg and Hamilton, Nico Hülkenberg was third on 28 points, with Fernando Alonso and Jenson Button on 26 and 23 points respectively. In the Constructors Championship, Mercedes were in a league of their own with a lead of 67 points over second placed Force India.

Prior to the race weekend, Stefano Domenicali resigned from his position as Ferrari team principal citing the team's poor start to the season and their longest winless streak for 18 years. Domenicali was replaced by the President and CEO of Ferrari North America, Marco Mattiacci.

As per the previous year, tyre supplier Pirelli brought its white-banded medium compound tyre as the harder prime tyre and the yellow-banded soft compound tyre as the softer option tyre.

QUALIFYING

Qualifying took place under wet conditions, with all drivers either using intermediates or extreme wets. In Q1 most of the drivers chose Pirelli's extreme wet tyre. It was obviously pretty slippery on track as Nico Rosberg found as he spun off the track at Turn 6 in his Mercedes. Pastor Maldonado's Lotus had broken down in FP3 and could not be repaired in time for qualifying.

Rosberg soon made up for his earlier error to top the timesheets with a 1m 56.351s lap. Team mate Lewis Hamilton moved into second with a 1m 57.477s. Fernando Alonso moved his Ferrari into third with a time of 1m 57.030s, while Hamilton improved his to a 1m 56.450s and with 1 minute remaining in the session, Hamilton went even quicker with a 1m 55.516s. The top 6 at the end of Q1 were Hamilton, Hulkenberg, Vettel, Rosberg, Bottas and Ricciardo. The 6 drivers eliminated at the end of Q1 were: Gutierrez, Kobayashi, Bianchi, Ericsson, Chilton and Maldonado.

7 minutes into Q2, all 16 drivers were on track, and they were all on the intermediates. Rosberg was fastest with a 1m 55.613s, but Hamilton immediately beat that with a 1m 54.200s. Vettel then separated the two Mercedes' with a time of 1m 54.888s. The top 10 at the end of Q2 were Hamilton, Vettel, Rosberg, Ricciardo, Alonso, Bottas, Grosjean, Vergne, Massa and Hulkenberg with the 6 drivers eliminated at the end of Q2 being Räikkönen, Button, Kvyat, Sutil, Magnussen and Pérez.

In Q3 light rain was forecast for the rest of the session, so most drivers were on inters.

With 8 minutes to go, Vettel was fastest with a 1m 54.981s. Rosberg was next with a 1m 55.143s. A minute later and Hamilton topped the charts with a 1m 54.348s. 5 minutes to go and the order was Hamilton, Vettel, Rosberg, Ricciardo and Alonso. 3 minutes later and Rosberg was flying as was Ricciardo who went on to pip his team mate into 2nd while Rosberg made mistakes and failed to improve on his previous time. With less than a minute remaining, Rosberg spun coming out of the final corner. So the top 10 looked like this - Hamilton, Ricciardo, Vettel, Rosberg, Alonso, Massa, Bottas, Hulkenberg, Vergne and Grosjean. Hamilton had clinched his third pole position for the season and his 34th career pole position and as a result became the highest pole position British driver of all time, ahead of Jim Clark's record of 33.

QUALIFYING RESULT (Top 10)

Q3	Car No.	Driver (Constructor)	Q1 Time	Q2 Time	Q3 Time	Grid Pos.
1	**44**	**Lewis Hamilton** **Mercedes**	**1:55.516**	**1:54.029**	**1:53.860**	**1**
2	3	Daniel Ricciardo Red Bull	1:56.641	1:55.302	1:54.455	2
3	1	Sebastian Vettel Red Bull	1:55.926	1:54.499	1:54.960	3
4	6	Nico Rosberg Mercedes	1:56.058	1:55.294	1:55.143	4
5	14	Fernando Alonso Ferrari	1:56.961	1:55.765	1:55.637	5
6	19	Felipe Massa Williams	1:56.850	1:56.757	1:56.147	6
7	77	Valtteri Bottas Williams	1:56.501	1:56.253	1:56.282	7
8	27	Nico Hülkenberg Force India	1:55.913	1:56.847	1:56.366	8
9	25	Jean-Eric Vergne Toro Rosso	1:57.477	1:56.584	1:56.773	9
10	8	Romain Grosjean Lotus	1:58.411	1:56.407	1:57.079	10

Pastor Maldonado - failed to set a lap time within 107% of the fastest lap time set by Lewis Hamilton in Q1 but was later given permission to start the race by the stewards.

THE RACE

Hamilton pulled away from the start and increased his lead by about a second a lap in the early stages and was in cruise control for the rest of the race. He has been accused of being hard on his tyres in the past but he handled his tyres far better than any of his rivals and has had better fuel consumption than most other drivers all season so far. Rosberg meanwhile, found himself in 6th place after lap 1 and it showed that even with a car as dominant as the Mercedes clearly is, how much more difficult it is if a driver finds himself out of position. A loss of telemetry data to the pit wall before the race may have contributed to his poor start compounded by the Williams of Valtteri Bottas bouncing over his front wheel on the entry to the first corner and so he found himself behind Hamilton, Vettel, Alonso, Ricciardo and Massa on the first lap. Alonso pushed and shoved Vettel around the first lap, but was forced to settle into third in the opening stint. The Ferrari driver had leapt up to 3rd at the first corner with his usual trademark fast start, despite a coming to blows with his erstwhile team mate, Felipe Massa. Rosberg managed to get past Massa on lap 4 and leapfrogged Ricciardo at the first pit stops, he then overtook Vettel on lap 22 and then set off after Alonso.

Alonso, too, had jumped ahead of Vettel into second at the first pit stops and managed to stay there until his second and final stop on lap 33, although by now Rosberg had moved up to his tail. An earlier, final stop by Alonso, and an error by Rosberg on his in-lap gave Alonso a 5 second lead after Rosberg's final stop four laps later. But Rosberg was driving a Mercedes and he let loose the power of the engine over the succeeding 5 laps and serenely cruised past the Ferrari on the straight on lap 42, with 14 laps to go. That left Alonso 5 seconds ahead of Ricciardo and desperate to keep the Red Bull driver behind. He eventually held on to be 1.2 seconds ahead, even though he was suffering from degradation on his front tyres.

"It was a good weekend," said Alonso. "We did improve the car a little bit compared to the first three races, so we felt more competitive. Being in the podium is a nice surprise for us. I think I'm third in the championship behind these two guys. We didn't have the start of the season we would have liked but we are still in the fight."

As Hamilton rounded the last corner at the end of the 55th lap of the 56 lap race, the chequered flag was waved at him by mistake. Lewis carried on at race pace but according to Article 43.2 of the FIA Sporting Regulations this meant that the race had been officially ended and that in those circumstances the result must stand from the end of the previous lap. Unfortunately for Caterham's Kobayashi, this meant that his overtake on Bianchi on the final lap did not count. A strange turn of events when you take into account the technological prowess of Formula 1, but it shows that human error can still make for an interesting denouement. At the end, Lewis Hamilton was 18.6 seconds ahead of his biggest rival and team mate Nico Rosberg and had now closed the gap in the Championship to 4 points, despite winning 3 of the 4 opening races. It meant he had won 3 races in a row for the first time in his career and had written his first trilogy! The team had also had its 3rd 1-2 in a row. "I just can't believe how amazing the car is and how hard everyone's worked," Hamilton said on the podium. "After the start I was just really racing myself. I'm really happy Nico is up here with us. Great points for the team."

An obviously unhappy Sebastian Vettel was 5th, beaten by his team mate Ricciardo for the second race in a row. The world champion had refused a team order to let Ricciardo by in the middle of the race. After being beaten by Ricciardo in qualifying, Vettel had admitted that his team mate was outpacing him fair and square, and he was outpacing him again now in the race. Ricciardo was on Vettel's tail by lap 23, whereupon Red Bull ordered the German to let him by. "What tyres is he on?" Vettel asked over the radio. His race engineer told him that he was on the same tyres as he was, but had stopped later. "Tough luck," Vettel replied. He must be getting a bit tired of being instructed by his team to stay behind or, to let an Australian by, after the infamous 'Multi 21' (Red Bull's code for holding station) incident at last year's Malaysian Grand Prix, which he also ignored. However, he was unable to stop a fast running Australian passing him this time. It appeared as though Vettel tried his damndest to keep ahead, but on the more slippery outside line, he ran wide, allowing Ricciardo through. Vettel said he moved over to let his team-mate pass!

Ricciardo flew away from him after that and was more than 20 seconds clear at the end of the race as Vettel was forced to focus on keeping ahead of Force India's Nico Hülkenberg in 6th. Bottas took 7th, from Kimi Räikkönen, who has now been beaten by his team mate in all four of his races since his return to Ferrari. Force India's Sergio Pérez and Toro Rosso's Daniil Kvyat took the final points positions.

"That was not a perfect weekend for me," said an unhappy Rosberg after the race. "Too many things went wrong, beginning with a technical problem and a less than perfect job from me in qualifying. Today I didn't have any telemetry, so there was no communication from the car to the pits. My engineers couldn't see what was going on in my car and therefore they couldn't set up my clutch for the start. The clutch was completely in the wrong place, which is why I had a really bad start. I had some contact with Bottas in Turn 1 and I thought that was it. Luckily my car wasn't damaged and in the following laps the pace in the car seemed good, which meant I was able to climb some positions. To finish second in the end, on a weekend of damage limitation, is great."

CHINESE GRAND PRIX 2014 RACE RESULT

Pos.	No.	Driver (Constructor)	Laps	Time	Grid	Points
1	44	**Lewis Hamilton** **Mercedes**	54	1:33:28.338	1	25
2	6	Nico Rosberg Mercedes	54	+18.686	4	18
3	14	Fernando Alonso Ferrari	54	+25.765	5	15
4	3	Daniel Ricciardo Red Bull-Renault	54	+26.978	2	12
5	1	Sebastian Vettel Red Bull-Renault	54	+51.012	3	10
6	27	Nico Hülkenberg Force India-Mercedes	54	+57.581	8	8
7	77	Valtteri Bottas Williams-Mercedes	54	+58.145	7	6
8	7	Kimi Räikkönen Ferrari	54	+1:23.990	11	4
9	11	Sergio Pérez Force India-Mercedes	54	+1:26.489	16	2
10	26	Daniil Kvyat Toro Rosso-Renault	53	+1 Lap	13	1

DRIVERS' CHAMPIONSHIP

Pos. Driver   Points

1	**Nico Rosberg**	**79**
2	Lewis Hamilton	75
3	Fernando Alonso	41
4	Nico Hülkenberg	36
5	Sebastian Vettel	33

CONSTRUCTORS' CHAMPIONSHIP

Pos. Constructor   Points

1	**Mercedes**	**154**
2	Red Bull-Renault	57
3	Force India-Mercedes	54
4	Ferrari	52
5	McLaren-Mercedes	43

THE SPANISH GRAND PRIX

BARCELONA

ROUND 5
CIRCUIT DE BARCELONA-CATALUNYA
SPANISH GRAND PRIX

4 SILVER ARROWS TO THE HEART

ONE MORE LAP AND I COULD HAVE GIVEN IT A GOOD GO

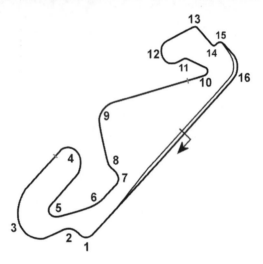

Date: 11 May 2014

Official Name: Formula 1 Gran Premio de España Pirelli 2014

Circuit: Circuit de Barcelona-Catalunya, Montmeló, Spain

Lap Length: 4.7 km (2.9 miles)

Lap Record: 1m 21.670s - Kimi Räikkönen (2008)

Distance: 66 laps, 307.024 km (190.826 miles)

The gap between lead drivers Nico Rosberg and Lewis Hamilton is now almost negligible at only 4 points with Fernando Alonso trailing in their wake, some 34 points behind Hamilton. But can Hamilton finally overhaul his team mate after his retirement in Australia has meant he has been playing catch-up ever since or can Rosberg stop the Hamilton machine from inflicting further damage? Tyre supplier Pirelli brought 2 different tyre compounds for the race - the hard primes and the medium option.

QUALIFYING

4 minutes into Q1, Pastor Maldonado crashed his Lotus at Turn 3, and ripped up the right front suspension. The red flags came out to stop the session. I don't know about you, but I don't know if Maldonado is just the recipient of tremendous and continuous bad luck or if he is just completely incompetent. He certainly is consistently on the wrong side of the stewards through either just daft driving or sometimes, extremely dangerous driving. I can't see why Lotus have kept faith with him for so long. After 7 minutes the green lights are back on to signal the restart.

With 10 minutes remaining in the session, Nico Rosberg took the lead with a time of 1m 26.764s. It is now really important for Nico to lay down a marker to gain some kind of psychological advantage over his team mate. Lewis Hamilton then took his Mercedes up to second ahead of Sebastian Vettel's Red Bull. So far all the top drivers are on hard compound tyres. The top 6 at the end of Q1 are Rosberg who did what was required and set down a marker, Hamilton, Vettel, Ricciardo, Massa and Kvyat, who again shows his potential in qualifying. The 6 drivers who are out are Sutil, Chilton, Bianchi, Ericsson, Kobayashi and, surprise of all surprises, Maldonado.

7 minutes into Q2, Massa set the fastest time with a 1m 27.733s, but Kimi Räikkönen beat that with a 1m 27.454s in his Ferrari. Everybody was on the medium tyres except for Jenson Button. Rosberg set his second marker of Qualifying with a 1m 26.088s and Hamilton took 2nd with a 1m 26.210s. Red Bull team mates Daniel Ricciardo and Sebastian Vettel moved up to 3rd and 4th respectively. With only 4 minutes remaining, everybody was in the pits except Hulkenberg. The top four guys did not need to run again, but those outside the top 10 or just above had to go again. With 2 minutes to go, the action was about to begin. Massa, 9th, went to fourth.

His teammate Valtteri Bottas, 10th, moved up to 8th. Button made it into the top 10, finally getting 9th, while Fernando Alonso just scraped into 10th place. The top 10 at the end of Q2 are Rosberg, Hamilton, Ricciardo, Massa, Vettel, Grosjean, Räikkönen, Bottas and Alonso. The 6 drivers who are out are Hulkenberg, Pérez, Kvyat, Gutierrez, Magnussen and Vergne. The last 2 not even setting a time in Q2. Vergne is due a 10 place grid penalty because the team had not properly secured a rear wheel during practice on Friday.

So the question is, can Rosberg now stop the qualifying rot and set down a even more significant marker for the race? Can he do it when it really matters? Rosberg was the first out. Hamilton followed him. Bottas was third out. All on the softer medium prime tyres. 4 minutes into the session and Vettel stops at Turn 3, complaining that his Red Bull had no drive. The red flags came out and the session is stopped. After a 5 minute delay Q3 resumes. Again Rosberg was first out. Hamilton, Ricciardo and Alonso join him. The other six drivers remained in their garages. With 5 minutes left, Rosberg set a 1m 26.288s lap, immediately countered by Hamilton with a 1m 26.561s. Ricciardo was 3rd with a 1m 26.602s while Alonso was 4th with 1m 27.563s. In their final runs, Rosberg improved to a 1m 25.400s to retake pole, but Hamilton again came back with a 1m 25.400s. Ricciardo was still in 3rd, while the race for 4th was on. Räikkönen took it first, then Grosjean and finally Bottas. So Hamilton does it again when it mattered and at the moment seems almost unstoppable. The top 10 qualifiers at the end of Q3 were Hamilton, Rosberg, Ricciardo, Bottas, Grosjean, Räikkönen, Alonso, Button, Massa and Vettel.

QUALIFYING RESULT (Top 10)

Q3	Car No.	Driver (Constructor)	Q1 Time	Q2 Time	Q3 Time	Grid Pos.
1	**44**	**Lewis Hamilton** **Mercedes**	**1:27.238**	**1:26.210**	**1:25.232**	**1**
2	6	Nico Rosberg Mercedes	1:26.764	1:26.088	1:25.400	2
3	3	Daniel Ricciardo Red Bull	1:28.053	1:26.613	1:26.285	3
4	77	Valtteri Bottas Williams	1:28.198	1:27.563	1:26.632	4
5	8	Romain Grosjean Lotus	1:28.472	1:27.258	1:26.960	5
6	7	Kimi Räikkönen Ferrari	1:28.308	1:27.335	1:27.104	5
7	14	Fernando Alonso Ferrari	1:28.329	1:27.602	1:27.140	6
8	22	Jenson Button McLaren	1:28.279	1:27.570	1:27.335	7
9	19	Felipe Massa Williams	1:28.061	1:27.016	1:27.402	8
10	1	Sebastian Vettel Red Bull	1:27.958	1:27.052	no time	15

Sebastian Vettel - 5 place grid penalty for an unscheduled gearbox change after qualifying.

Jean-Éric Vergne - 10 place grid penalty for an unsafe pit release in FP2.

Pastor Maldonado - failed to set a lap time during qualifying. He was allowed to participate in the race by the race stewards.

THE RACE

Hamilton again started well from pole and led until he made his first pit stop, pulling out a lead of some 2.6 seconds. Rosberg inherited the lead for 4 laps before pitting himself. Hamilton was back out in front from laps 22 to 43 before making his final stop. After two laps in first, Rosberg handed the position back to Hamilton on lap 46. The gap between them was now around 3.6 seconds.

As the Mercedes' drivers disappeared out of sight, Ricciardo had lost a place to Bottas at the start but the Red Bull was faster and Ricciardo jumped ahead at the first set of stops. Vettel was recovering well after his 5 place grid penalty after a gearbox failure. Red Bull put him on a 3 stop strategy for the race, and after his final stop on lap 52 he immediately overtook Räikkönen and then subsequently passed Bottas on lap 63. Alonso, who was behind his team mate Räikkönen, was planning to make 2 stops, but switched to 3 in an attempt to get ahead of his team mate and Vettel but he failed to get ahead of the latter when he was slowed by traffic on his out-lap. In the first stint, Alonso had been frustrated by being stuck behind Grosjean and Räikkönen, who were both slower.

Alonso was now closer to his team mate and after a few laps of failing to get past him on the main straight, he tried the outside of Turn 1 on lap 64, cut back into Turn 2, followed Räikkönen through the fast Turn 3 and to the delight of his home fans out-braked his team mate into Turn 4.

At the second pit stops, Hamilton and Rosberg went in opposite directions, with Hamilton switching to the primes for the middle stint and then to the mediums for the last stint while Rosberg went for the mediums and then the primes. "There was a misunderstanding from my side," Rosberg said, "because we were going to go prime second stint, there were two variables. There was one where we go prime second stint if we have graining in the first stint. Or I go prime second stint to try and beat Lewis if I feel that pace-wise I can be quicker and have a shot at it. I thought they were going prime because they thought I had graining, but I didn't have graining, so that's why I was confused, but then I understood. It was to offset my strategy so that I would have a chance to fight Lewis at the end so it was fine, and just what I wanted."

Meanwhile, Räikkönen questioned Ferrari's strategy on the radio as he slowed down after the race, "who made these calls," and that he, "seemed to be getting second choice". Räikkönen admitted that he had, "wanted to clarify a few things." Behind, Grosjean took Lotus' first points of the season in 8th, ahead of the Force Indias of Pérez and Hulkenberg.

Up front, Rosberg had saved his tyres and then closed in on Hamilton. On lap 63 he had got the gap down to 0.9 seconds. Then 0.6 seconds. But he still couldn't get close enough to overtake. "This is a really, really difficult track to get close to the guy in front." Rosberg said, "I still got close, y'know Turn 10, the last lap. Could have got gone for a kamikaze move but it wouldn't have worked. Lewis did a great job the whole weekend and was just that little bit ahead. But there are a lot of positives for me to take out of it. I'm fully motivated to just try to get that little bit extra and to edge him out next time - and it's doable."

Rosberg, commenting on the close finish, said, "One more and I could have given it a good go. I wasn't close enough to give it a go there, but next lap I would have, but unfortunately that was it! I'm a bit gutted but second place means it is still close in the championship, and many more races to go yet."

At the chequered flag Lewis was just 0.636 ahead of Nico and had now won 4 races in a row and 26 for his career and was now leading the World Championship by 3 points. The first time this season that he has led. "It's very difficult to really put into words the feeling when you come to a race and have a result like this. Never have I had a car like this and obviously we've never had a gap like this to anyone before. Nico did a fantastic job today, it was a struggle to keep him behind. I just feel that it is such a huge blessing, for not only me but for all the guys in the team, because of all the hard work they've done for many years now, but finally they are starting to see the fruits of their labour. I'm just enjoying every moment, every step of the way. I wasn't fast enough really today, Nico was quicker. I struggled a lot with the balance and really had to rely on my engineers a lot more to give me the gaps and to try to find where I could find time. And also with all my settings, I was moving them up and down, up and down, really trying to find extra time. But Nico was just generally quicker this weekend but fortunately I was able to keep him behind."

"The race was really lost in qualifying and at the start," Rosberg said. "Those were the two opportunities I had. Qualifying was very, very close, I even had a bit of a problem which we found in hindsight, where I was a little bit down on power on the straight, but the difference was not enough to get pole, but still it was actually even closer than it looked. And then just had a poor start, so those were the two shots that I had at it and it didn't work out."

Ricciardo was a distant 50 seconds behind the invisible Mercedes to gain the first podium of his career. "Not exactly the start I wanted. I think initially the launch felt OK but we lost a bit of traction after that. Bottas got past me. The first stint I tried to hang in there, had, let's say, a pseudo-attempt into Turn One. I got underneath him but it wasn't deep enough to pull the move off and then, yeah, it was just about doing an undercut and just trying to still make a two-stop work. So from then on it was a pretty lonely race. Unfortunately we're not going to catch Mercedes. At least this weekend we weren't going to, so a lonely third was not a bad result in the end."

Bottas was running in 4th, but Vettel took that from him with 4 laps to go.

"The strategy was correct and the team did really well in the pit stops," Bottas said. "I made no mistake on the track so we made the maximum of what was on offer and got some good points from it. It's pleasing to be in the points and it equals my best ever result. It was a shame Vettel was so quick at the end, I tried to defend, but he had fresher tyres. The atmosphere in the team is fantastic, we are all pushing forward and points feed that hunger."

Vettel seemed pleased with himself after recovering from his 5 place grid penalty. "The start was not so great and I lost a place," Vettel said, "but then I was able to get it back towards the end of the lap, it's always tricky when you are further back. It was a very busy first lap. I was then sort of stuck in the train, so I couldn't really feel how far we could go today and how quick we were, but once we came in I was on the harder tyre and was able to stick with the people in front and even catch them a little bit. I think we realized that the pace was there and after that we had two fresh sets of tyres from yesterday, so we could go even further up the road."

SPANISH GRAND PRIX 2014 RACE RESULT

Pos.	No.	Driver (Constructor)	Laps	Time	Grid	Points
1	44	**Lewis Hamilton** **Mercedes**	**66**	**1:41:05.155**	1	**25**
2	6	Nico Rosberg Mercedes	66	+0.636	2	18
3	3	Daniel Ricciardo Red Bull-Renault	66	+49.014	3	15
4	1	Sebastian Vettel Red Bull-Renault	66	+1:16.702	15	12
5	77	Valtteri Bottas Williams-Mercedes	66	+1:19.293	4	10
6	14	Fernando Alonso Ferrari	66	+1:27.743	7	8
7	7	Kimi Räikkönen Ferrari	65	+1 Lap	6	6
8	8	Romain Grosjean Lotus-Renault	65	+1 Lap	5	4
9	11	Sergio Pérez Force India-Mercedes	65	+1 Lap	11	2
10	27	Nico Hülkenberg Force India-Mercedes	65	+1 Lap	10	1

DRIVERS' CHAMPIONSHIP

Pos.	Driver	Points
1	**Lewis Hamilton**	**100**
2	Nico Rosberg	97
3	Fernando Alonso	49
4	Sebastian Vettel	45
5	Daniel Ricciardo	39

CONSTRUCTORS' CHAMPIONSHIP

Pos.	Constructor	Points
1	**Mercedes**	**197**
2	Red Bull-Renault	84
3	Ferrari	66
4	Force India-Mercedes	57
5	Williams-Mercedes	46

THE MONACO GRAND PRIX

MONTE CARLO

ROUND 6
CIRCUIT DE MONACO
MONACO GRAND PRIX

GRIT IN YOUR EYE
ROSBERG DOMINATES IN MONTE CARLO

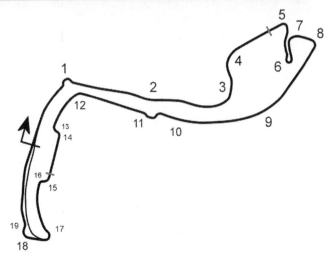

Date: 25 May 2014

Official Name: Formula 1 Grand Prix de Monaco 2014

Circuit: Circuit de Monaco, La Condamine and Monte Carlo, Monaco - Temporary street circuit

Lap Length: 3.3 km (2.1 miles)

Lap Record: 1m 14.439s - Michael Schumacher (2004)

Distance: 78 laps, 260.5 km (161.9 miles)

The nervous tension at Mercedes has been notched up a few points when it transpired that Hamilton was found to have used a higher powered engine setting than the team allowed during the latter stages of the Spanish Grand Prix, in his attempt to stay ahead of his team mate. Then it came out that Rosberg had done a similar thing in Bahrain in his attempt to get past Hamilton.

Tyre supplier Pirelli brought its yellow-marked soft compound tyre as the harder prime tyre and the red-marked super-soft compound tyre as the softer option tyre, the same combination that has been in the past two years.

QUALIFYING

In Q1 Rosberg was the first out in his Mercedes and he set down a fairly decent time of 1m 17.938s, while his team mate did a 1m 18.751s, both set on the harder soft tyres. A few minutes later and Daniil Kvyat lost control of his Toro Rosso coming out of the chicane and he spun straight into the barrier. With 8 minutes to go, Ricciardo on the softs moved to third ahead of Romain Grosjean who was on the super softs. A few minutes later and Kevin Magnussen ran straight on in Turn 1. Meanwhile his team mate, Jenson Button moved into third place. In the final minute of Q1 Vergne moved his Toro Rosso into the top spot, while Ericsson slid into Massa's Williams at Mirabeau. Q1 top 6 were Vergne, Rosberg, Hamilton, Alonso, Button and Ricciardo. Drivers that were out were Gutierrez, Sutil, Bianchi, Chilton, Kobayashi and Ericsson.

In Q2 Ricciardo set the early marker with a 1m 17.769s which he later lowered to a 1m 17.233s. Rosberg and Hamilton reacted with times of 1m 16.682s and 1m 16.717s while the Ferraris of Alonso and Räikkönen were 4th and 5th. After a bad first run, Vettel jumped to 4th with a 1m 17.302s with 6 minutes to go. With less than one minute remaining, Hamilton took top spot with a 1m 16.354s. The top 10 were Hamilton, Rosberg, Vettel, Ricciardo, Räikkönen, Kvyat, Magnussen, Vergne and Pérez. The 6 out were Hulkenberg, Button, Bottas, Grosjean, Maldonado and Massa.

Now comes the crunch. It is extremely difficult to overtake on the tight, twisting Monaco circuit, with very little room to place the car in the few places that overtaking is viable, especially with the unforgiving barriers waiting to claim you if you make the slightest mistake - as a consequence pole position is king. 5 minutes into the session, Alonso sets a 1m 16.792s. Rosberg immediately responds with a 1m 15.989s while Hamilton could only manage a 1m 16.048s. With 4 minutes left Ricciardo was 3rd and Vettel 4th followed by Alonso, Räikkönen, Vergne, Magnussen, Pérez Kvyat. On the final runs Rosberg locks his brakes approaching Mirabeau and then runs up the escape road, it's over for him. But what about Hamilton - he's behind Rosberg and is going faster but the Yellow flags are out at Mirabeau following Rosberg's error and Lewis is forced to slow down under yellows as he passes his stricken team mate and it's all over. Rosberg has the all important pole position. So the top 10 are Rosberg, Hamilton, Ricciardo, Vettel, Alonso, Räikkönen, Vergne, Magnussen, Kvyat and Pérez.

"Not the way I want it," Rosberg said. "I thought I had ruined it. But I am happy with pole, it's fantastic and I hope for more tomorrow. I definitively disadvantaged Lewis and the others, but it was a genuine mistake. Of course I'm sorry for Lewis I didn't know where he was. Of course it's not great. It's not an ideal way to end qualifying. I thought it was over - I thought the track would ramp up and someone else could beat my time. I'm happy it worked out. Pole at home is fantastic - it couldn't be better."

Hamilton was not particularly impressed with Rosberg's antics. "There isn't much to say," he said, "the damage was done. I was a couple of tenths up before the yellow flag. I'll just have a look later. Yes, it's ironic to get pole position by going off..."

QUALIFYING RESULT (Top 10)

Q3	Car No.	Driver (Constructor)	Q1 Time	Q2 Time	Q3 Time	Grid Pos.
1	**6**	**Nico Rosberg** **Mercedes**	**1:17.678**	**1:16.465**	**1:15.989**	**1**
2	44	Lewis Hamilton Mercedes	1:17.823	1:16.354	1:16.048	2
3	3	Daniel Ricciardo Red Bull	1:17.900	1:17.233	1:16.384	3
4	1	Sebastian Vettel Red Bull	1:18.383	1:17.074	1:16.547	4
5	14	Fernando Alonso Ferrari	1:17.853	1:17.200	1:16.686	5
6	7	Kimi Räikkönen Ferrari	1:17.902	1:17.398	1:17.389	6
7	25	Jean-Eric Vergne Toro Rosso	1:17.557	1:17.657	1:17.540	7
8	20	Kevin Magnussen McLaren	1:17.978	1:17.609	1:17.555	8
9	26	Daniil Kvyat Toro Rosso	1:18.616	1:17.594	1:18.090	9
10	11	Sergio Pérez Force India	1:18.108	1:17.755	1:18.327	10

Jules Bianchi - five-place grid penalty, for an unscheduled gearbox change.

Marcus Ericsson started from the pit lane after causing a collision with Felipe Massa in Q1.

THE RACE

Monaco is one of the best circuits to see the cars in action. It seems almost impossible for the circuit to hold a Formula 1 race. It's tight nature and slow twisting sections and the closeness of the treacherous barriers make the drivers appear to be on the very edge, which they are. The circuit doesn't allow for too much overtaking, so some races can be a procession and the grid can often end up as the finishing positions. Throw in some rain and you have a different story and we've had some great races in the past when the track is wet. Monaco, in some way, is the heart of Formula 1, simply because it sums up the glamour, the wealth and the draw of the sport as the rich and famous flock to see one of the social events of the year.

Given the circuit's nature, you can understand how Lewis was feeling after qualifying. The question in the paddock is whether Nico did it on purpose or was it a mistake, and the general consensus is that he did it on purpose. However, the stewards felt no action was necessary and left it at that. Personally, at the time, I thought it was a genuine mistake and that he took to the escape road in order to avoid slamming into the barriers by attempting to take the corner. If it was on purpose in order to scupper Lewis' chance of beating his time, as he himself was not improving on his best time, then it seems that it was a pretty risky manoeuvre, as he easily could have put it in the barriers and then struggled to make the grid on Sunday. It also seems a little out of character for Nico, who appears to be a well-mannered, personable guy, unless he does have a disguised ruthless streak under that amiable exterior. At the time I thought the yellows were a little excessive as he was quite a way from the track down the escape road. Some suggested that they could have red flagged the session and restarted it when the car was removed, allowing all those drivers who had their final run compromised to have another shot at it and I think that would have been the best solution and I also think it's a possibility that the FIA should look into for the future. However, having looked at the incident again and again I'm not so sure that he didn't do it on purpose, it does seem that his reaction to the lockup was a bit soft and that he could have carried on. Martin Brundle said a similar thing, saying that he felt that at first he thought it was a mistake by Nico but that he had started to change his mind, knowing how important pole position is at Monaco and how much Nico needed to stop Lewis' winning streak.

After all is said and done, I think that proved to be a major turning point which Nico definitely benefitted from. It seemed as if for the first time Nico had got under Lewis' skin. It was obvious that Lewis was fuming over the incident.

Pastor Maldonado stalled on the grid before the warm-up lap, and failed to start the race. At the start, Rosberg led from Lewis Hamilton with Sebastian Vettel behind. Räikkönen jumped from 6th to 4th, ahead of Ricciardo and team mate Alonso who had been trapped behind Ricciardo off the grid. On lap 1, Pérez ran a little wide at Mirabeau and as he returned to the racing ling was hit by Button's McLaren. Pérez spun and collided with Sutil and Grosjean. The safety car was deployed and Pérez retired, as did Vettel who had turbo problems.

After his earlier collision with Pérez, Sutil moved up from the back of the field, but on lap 23 at the Nouvelle chicane, he lost the car coming out of the tunnel and hit the barriers causing the safety car to be deployed for the second time. Everyone pitted under the safety car except Felipe Massa. After the restart, Räikkönen received a puncture after being hit by Chilton and dropped to the back of the field. Gutierrez hit the barrier at La Rascasse on lap 59 and had to retire due to damage to his rear suspension while in 8th. Bianchi was now in 10th, giving him the opportunity to score Marussia's first points in Formula 1. However, he received a 5 second penalty for illegally taking an earlier 5 second penalty when the safety car was out.

Meanwhile, Hamilton had been consistently around a second behind Rosberg for almost all of the race with Ricciardo 15 seconds further behind. With 12 laps remaining Hamilton complained of having some dirt in his eye and consequently began to slow, allowing Ricciardo to close in on him. At one point his team radioed him about the Ricciardo situation and he snapped back that he didn't care about Ricciardo, but wanted to know how far Nico was ahead. He seemed oblivious to the fact that his 2nd place was now in jeopardy. "This is such a difficult circuit to overtake," Hamilton said. "I was following Nico as close as I could and had great pace but I just couldn't get past. Towards the end, I got some dirt in my eye through the visor which made it very tough for a few laps but thankfully it cleared up and I was able to hold off Daniel and keep second place. This hasn't been the greatest of weekends but I'll go into the next race with even more energy and determination."

Rosberg's win in the Monaco Grand Prix was his second in a row at the famous circuit and he went back into the lead of the drivers' championship.

Alonso, in fourth, was the only other car to finish on the lead lap. Hulkenberg was 5th, after fending off a late charge from Button who was on fresher rubber. Massa was 7th, ahead of Grosjean and Bianchi. Bianchi dropped to 9th after his 5 second penalty was added to his race time, still earning Marussia their first ever points in Formula 1.

Rosberg said of his race win, "The race started well and I was comfortable but then we had to manage my fuel consumption and Lewis was pushing really hard behind me. We were able to be in control of the fuel with a few laps of lift and coast. It was important for me to break Lewis' momentum of winning the last four races, this weekend. That worked out very well, but it was a really tough weekend. I'm so happy for the team that we had another one-two finish and look forward to the party tonight!"

On the podium it was clear that Hamilton was still fuming and he hardly even looked at Rosberg. "Generally, there is a fierce battle between me and Nico and it will continue that way too, I'm sure quite late in the season," he said. "Nico has not had a single hiccup through the season so far. Obviously I had a car that didn't finish in Melbourne but otherwise it's still quite close, so I'm just going to keep my head up, keep pushing. I know the team are working hard for the both of us. The team can sometimes be in awkward positions, which they were yesterday, and their job is really to protect us both and that's what they did."

MONACO GRAND PRIX 2014 RACE RESULT

Pos.	No.	Driver (Constructor)	Laps	Time	Grid	Points
1	6	**Nico Rosberg** **Mercedes**	78	1:49:27.661	1	25
2	44	Lewis Hamilton Mercedes	78	+9.210	2	18
3	3	Daniel Ricciardo Red Bull-Renault	78	+9.614	3	15
4	14	Fernando Alonso Ferrari	78	+32.452	5	12
5	27	Nico Hülkenberg Force India-Mercedes	77	+1 Lap	11	10
6	22	Jenson Button McLaren-Mercedes	77	+1 Lap	12	8
7	19	Felipe Massa Williams-Mercedes	77	+1 Lap	16	6
8	8	Romain Grosjean Lotus-Renault	77	+1 Lap	14	4
9	17	Jules Bianchi Marussia-Ferrari	77	+1 Lap	21	2
10	20	Kevin Magnussen McLaren-Mercedes	77	+1 Lap	8	1

Jules Bianchi - 5 seconds was added to his race time for serving a penalty under the safety car.

DRIVERS' CHAMPIONSHIP

Pos.   Driver   Points

1   **Nico Rosberg**   **122**
2   Lewis Hamilton   118
3   Fernando Alonso   61
4   Daniel Ricciardo   54
5   Nico Hülkenberg   47

CONSTRUCTORS' CHAMPIONSHIP

Pos.	Constructor	Points
1	**Mercedes**	**240**
2	Red Bull-Renault	99
3	Ferrari	78
4	Force India-Mercedes	67
5	McLaren-Mercedes	52

THE CANADIAN GRAND PRIX

MONTREAL

ROUND 7
CIRCUIT GILLES VILLENEUVE
CANADIAN GRAND PRIX

AUSTRALIAN RULES

MERCEDES' DOMINANCE FINALLY BROKEN

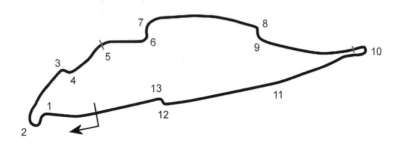

Date: 8 June 2014

Official Name: Formula 1 Grand Prix du Canada 2014

Circuit: Circuit Gilles Villeneuve, Montreal, Canada - Temporary street circuit

Lap Length: 4.4 km (2.7 miles)

Lap Record: 1m 13.622s - Rubens Barrichello (2004)

Distance: 70 laps, 305.3 km (189.7 miles)

Tyre supplier Pirelli brought its yellow-banded soft compound tyre as the harder prime tyre and the red-banded supersoft compound tyre as the softer option tyre. The previous year medium and super-soft compound were used. The race was Kimi Räikkönen's 200th Grand Prix.

QUALIFYING

Williams team mates Valtteri Bottas and Felipe Massa had been quick in FP3, and were fancied to do well in qualifying. Nico Rosberg set the early pace with a 1m 16.690s lap. Lewis Hamilton responded with a 1m 16.438s. With 9 minutes gone, the top four were Hamilton, Rosberg, Massa and Bottas, with the Williams' pair fulfilling their free practice promise. Hamilton then improved to 1m 15.750s. The top drivers were all on soft tyres to save their super softs for later. 2 minutes to go and Daniil Kvyat leaped to 6th in his Toro Rosso while Maldonado makes a mistake and takes to the escape road. The top 10 in Q1 were Hamilton, Magnussen, Rosberg, Button, Massa, Bottas, Hulkenberg, Kvyat, Alonso and Räikkönen. The 6 out were Maldonado, Chilton, Bianchi, Kobayashi, Ericsson and Gutierrez.

In Q2, the Williams' pairing were first to make a mark, Bottas with a 1m 15.924s, and Massa with a 1m 15.773s. Alonso and Räikkönen moved into 3rd and 4th. Ricciardo then slotted his Red Bull into 4th, which became 5th as Rosberg did a 1m 15.832s to go behind Massa. Hamilton went 3rd with a 1m 15.882s. Sebastian Vettel was on the cusp in 11th. Massa and Bottas were 1st and 2nd until Rosberg does a 1m 15.289 to go 1st and then Hamilton beats it with a 1m 15.054s. Top 10 after Q2 were Hamilton, Rosberg, Massa, Bottas, Ricciardo, Vettel, Alonso, Button, Räikkönen and Vergne. The 6 drivers who missed the cut were Hulkenberg, Magnussen, Pérez, Grosjean, Kvyat and Sutil.

It took 2 minutes into Q3 before anyone ventured onto the track when Bottas took to the empty track. A couple of minutes later several drivers joined him. Bottas set a 1m 15.550s. Rosberg a 1m 14.946 with Hamilton just behind with a 1m 15.014s. Massa was 4th with a 1m 15.621s. Ricciardo and Vettel were 5th and 6th. Final runs began with 3 minutes left. With less than a minute to go, Rosberg did a great lap to grab pole position of 1m 14.874s as Hamilton's could only do a 1m 14.953s. Vettel was 3rd. So the order for the grid was Rosberg, Hamilton, Vettel, Bottas, Massa, Ricciardo, Alonso, Vergne, Button and Räikkönen.

QUALIFYING RESULT (Top 10)

Q3	Car No.	Driver (Constructor)	Q1 Time	Q2 Time	Q3 Time	Grid Pos.
1	6	**Nico Rosberg Mercedes**	**1:16.471**	**1:15.289**	**1:14.874**	1
2	44	Lewis Hamilton Mercedes	1:15.750	1.15.054	1:14.953	2
3	1	Sebastian Vettel Red Bull	1:17.470	1:16.109	1:15.548	3
4	77	Valtteri Bottas Williams	1:16.772	1:15.806	1:15.550	4
5	19	Felipe Massa Williams	1:16.666	1:15.773	1:15.578	5
6	3	Daniel Ricciardo Red Bull	1:17.113	1:15.897	1:15.589	6
7	14	Fernando Alonso Ferrari	1:17.010	1:16.131	1:15.814	7
8	25	Jean-Eric Vergne Toro Rosso	1:17.178	1:16.255	1:16.162	8
9	22	Jenson Button McLaren	1:16.631	1:16.214	1:16.182	9
10	7	Kimi Räikkönen Ferrari	1:17.013	1:16.245	1:16.214	10

Kamui Kobayashi - 5 place grid penalty for an unscheduled gearbox change.

Esteban Gutiérrez - unable to take part in qualifying as a result of a crash during FP3. He was allowed to start the race on the stewards' discretion as he was deemed capable of lapping with the 107% limit based on his free practice times. A further penalty ensued because his car needed a gearbox and a survival cell change, which meant he had to start from the pit lane.

THE RACE

Would the Mercedes' dominance of the season continue on? Is it possible that it could be a complete whitewash for the first time in Formula 1 history? The answer to both questions was given at the Canadian Grand Prix and the answer was a resounding 'no' to both questions. Even when Vettel managed to sneak into 2nd place at the start while Hamilton and Rosberg concentrated on each other, Mercedes were still likely to come in 1-2. On the first lap there was a huge accident between the Marussia teammates of Chilton and Bianchi as Chilton sent Bianchi into the wall at Turns 3 and 4. "I got a great start and kept everyone who was behind me, behind and then obviously Max and I were racing each other through Turns 2 and 3. I braked into Turn 3 and there was an impact, after which I ended up in the wall with a badly damaged car," Bianchi said. Chilton was given a 3 place grid penalty for the next race. With the safety car out, the order was Rosberg, Vettel, Hamilton, Bottas Massa and Ricciardo. Hamilton then passed Vettel and the established order was restored, with Hamilton 1.7 seconds behind Rosberg. They were the last to pit after the first short stint, on the softer tyres. Hamilton closed the gap to about half a second after the pit stops. On a different strategy, the Force India guys were 3rd and 4th with Pérez ahead of Hulkenberg. Vettel was 5th, Bottas 6th and Ricciardo 7th.

At the half distance point the unexpected happened, when almost simultaneously Lewis and Rosberg reported a loss of power, which was effecting their braking. Hamilton still manages to close the gap on Rosberg, and tries to take him on the outside of Turn 12, at the pit entrance, but locks up and runs wide - he is really struggling with his brakes! Then Hamilton has to pit and subsequently they retire the car. Rosberg kept going albeit at a severely reduced pace. Toto Wolff, the Mercedes Motorsport Director said, "I feel very sorry for Lewis. First of all, I must say his retirement was not his fault in any way and it is something the team has to take on the chin. Both drivers were doing a great job up to the point when the MGU-K failed. That also led to the brake failure that forced Lewis to retire after the second pit stop." On lap 46 Massa, after Rosberg pitted for the 2nd time, was now leading (although he had yet to pit for a second time, the first time this year that any car other than the Mercedes had led a race.) Rosberg said, "I lost the ERS and when you lose ERS then it doesn't harvest anymore, and then all the braking on the rear is being done by the brakes and then the rear brakes overheated. So it was one problem and then the next problem happened. That just made it massively difficult. I needed to cool the brakes a lot. I lost a lot of power on the straights. At the same time, taking those things into consideration, I was just pushing flat out, qualifying laps, one after another and managing to stay ahead of that pack behind me until two laps from the end."

After the pit stop phase had ended Rosberg was ahead of the field by only a second over Pérez. Ricciardo had now leapfrogged Vettel after the pit stops and was 3rd. 4 seconds behind this close group was another group of Hulkenberg, Bottas, Massa and Alonso. Pérez had managed to be in amongst the lead cars because he had only pitted once and although he was quick, Ricciardo was closing him down and finally passed him on lap 66. He was now on the hunt for Rosberg who had recovered somewhat from his earlier issue but was still well short of his optimum speed. With only 2 laps remaining Ricciardo easily overtook Rosberg to lead the race. "The race really came to life in the last 15 to 20 laps," Ricciardo said. "We saw Hamilton had a problem and then we saw Rosberg was slow on the straights. I was really struggling to get past Pérez. They had a pretty good car on the straights and he was holding me off well in the corners. We finally got a run out of the last chicane and made a nice move into turn and then set my sights on Nico and then a couple of laps to go just found myself in the right spot to get the DRS."

Vettel caught up with Pérez who was in 3rd and on the final lap, Felipe Massa tried to do the same but as they approached Turn 1 Massa attempted to pass Pérez on the inside. Pérez appeared to move very slightly across his line which took Massa by surprise and they touched, and both were out control as they careered along the track towards the barriers at full speed, hitting them with tremendous force. The safety car came out to pace the cars for the final lap and the race finished under those conditions, to be only the 6th race in Formula 1 history to finish under the safety car. "Finishing under the safety car made it a bit weird," Ricciardo said, "but I wanted to make sure the two drivers who were in the accident were okay before I started celebrating. We achieved a great result today with first and third, so let's enjoy it, but we will still have some work to do also. This will motivate the guys to work even harder and find even more, so I'm sure it will keep coming even better for us at the next few races." He added, "I'm a Grand Prix winner! I think it still seems a bit surreal to be honest, just because it all happened so quickly at the end. I was third for a while and then it all happened in a really exciting fashion. Once I got past Pérez I knew I just had to drive clean and get in Rosberg's DRS zone and, from then on, it was just awesome. I'm still a bit in shock. Thanks everyone. This is ridiculous! Lots of Aussie flags, that's nice!"

Rosberg was a little more sanguine after his 2nd place finish, "That was a big battle all the way through today! I had a tough start but I was able to defend in the first few corners and fight against Lewis. The race went smoothly for a while then both cars suddenly lost the MGU-K system and a lot of power which was really tough. Then I lost some time in the second pit stop which let Lewis jump me and I was struggling to cool the rear brakes down so it was all happening. Towards the end of the race, I tried to defend against Sergio which was fine but Daniel was too fast on the straights with much more power than I had available and he was able to get past. With so much going on, I had to ask my engineer where I finished at the end as I thought I was probably about fifth or sixth. I was so happy to hear that I was in P2!"

On the last lap accident, Massa was livid with Pérez, "I was one of the quickest guys on the track, so we lost many points today. I'm happy that I'm here with no problems but I'm so disappointed for what happened with Pérez, and also for the pit stop because I think maybe we could even have fought for victory today."

Pérez, however refused to take the blame, "On the final lap I was defending my position going into turn one when I suddenly got hit from behind. It was a big impact, but I am okay. I'm really sad for the team because we had an amazing race today and the one-stop strategy was working perfectly. It was not easy in the final laps and I was pushing hard to try and get ahead of Nico for the lead. Daniel managed to get ahead of me when I had an electrical issue with my car, but I managed to reset the system for the final couple of laps. The podium was possible today and I'm just very disappointed for the points we have lost."

Race officials, however, did blame Pérez for causing the accident and he was given a 5 place grid penalty for the next race.

So for the first time this year, the Mercedes have been beaten - albeit due to mechanical problems. But that doesn't take away from Ricciardo's magnificent drive and he is now consistently getting the better of his more illustrious team mate. Meanwhile, with Hamilton's retirement, Rosberg stretches his lead at the top of the championship to 22 points, while Ricciardo's win moves him up to 3rd.

CANADIAN GRAND PRIX 2014 RACE RESULT

Pos.	No.	Driver (Constructor)	Laps	Time	Grid	Points
1	3	**Daniel Ricciardo** **Red Bull-Renault**	**70**	**1:39:12.830**	**6**	**25**
2	6	Nico Rosberg Mercedes	70	+4.236	1	18
3	1	Sebastian Vettel Red Bull-Renault	70	+5.247	3	15
4	22	Jenson Button McLaren-Mercedes	70	+11.755	9	12
5	27	Nico Hülkenberg Force India-Mercedes	70	+12.843	11	10
6	14	Fernando Alonso Ferrari	70	+14.869	7	8
7	77	Valtteri Bottas Williams-Mercedes	70	+23.578	4	6
8	25	Jean-Éric Vergne Toro Rosso-Renault	70	+28.026	8	4
9	20	Kevin Magnussen McLaren-Mercedes	70	+29.254	12	2
10	7	Kimi Räikkönen Ferrari	70	+53.678	10	1

DRIVERS' CHAMPIONSHIP

Pos. Driver   Points

1 **Nico Rosberg**   **140**
2 Lewis Hamilton   118
3 Daniel Ricciardo   79
4 Fernando Alonso   69
5 Sebastian Vettel   60

CONSTRUCTORS' CHAMPIONSHIP

Pos.	Constructor	Points
1	**Mercedes**	**258**
2	Red Bull-Renault	139
3	Ferrari	87
4	Force India-Mercedes	77
5	McLaren-Mercedes	66

THE AUSTRIAN GRAND PRIX

RED BULL RING

ROUND 8
THE RED BULL RING
AUSTRIAN GRAND PRIX

TEUTONIC ORDER RESTORED

ROSBERG GATHERING MOMENTUM

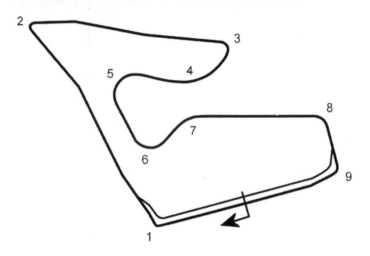

Date: 22 June 2014

Official Name: Formula 1 Großer Preis Von Österreich 2014

Circuit: Red Bull Ring, Spielberg, Styria, Austria

Lap Length: 4.3 km (2.7 miles)

Lap Record: 1m 08.337s - Michael Schumacher (2003)

Distance: 71 laps, 307.1 km (190.6 miles)

THE RETURN OF THE SILVER ARROWS

The renamed Red Bull Ring in the picturesque setting of the Mur Valley in South West Styria surrounded by the mountains of Styria, would host a Formula 1 race for the first time since 2003.

QUALIFYING

After 6 minutes of Q1, Alonso was leading with a 1m 10.671s, which was eclipsed by Hamilton with a 1m 09.762s, while Rosberg was 2nd with a 1m 10.124s. Many drivers including Bottas, Grosjean, Alonso and Kvyat were to have their times discounted by the strict track limits particularly at the Turn 1 'Castrol Edge' corner and at the penultimate Turn 8 'Rindt' corner, which was catching them by surprise. Massa put his Williams into 3rd with a time of 1m 10.292s. With 3 minutes to go Kvyat again proves fast in qualifying and was 2nd with Pérez in 5th. Top 6 in Q1 were Hamilton, Kvyat, Rosberg, Magnussen, Pérez and Jean-Eric Vergne. The 6 drivers who were out were Sutil, Gutierrez, Bianchi, Kobayashi, Chilton and Ericsson.

5 minutes into Q2 Magnussen went fastest with a 1m 09.524s. Massa beat him with a 1m 09.239s, soon after beaten by teammate Bottas 1m 09.096s. 3 minutes later Hamilton went top with a 1m 09.092 which Rosberg beat with a 1m 08.974s. In the last minute, Ricciardo, who was in danger of being eliminated squeezed in, in 9th, but Vettel was only 12th and out. Q2 top 10 were Rosberg, Hamilton, Bottas, Massa, Magnussen, Alonso, Kvyat, Hulkenberg, Ricciardo and Kimi Räikkönen. The 6 drivers eliminated were Pérez, Button, Vettel, Maldonado, Vergne and Grosjean. Pérez gets a 5-place grid penalty as his punishment for his collision with Massa in Canada, so will drop from 11th to 16th.

At the half way point of Q3, Bottas was fastest and Massa took 2nd with a 1m 09.150s. Both Mercedes' drivers were on track but Hamilton's exceeded the track limits at 'Rindt' while Rosberg moved into 2nd with a 1m 08.944s. Just before the final runs the order was Bottas, Rosberg, Massa, Alonso, Ricciardo, Magnussen with Hamilton only 9th. Under a minute left and Hamilton spins as he pushes too hard. Massa set a 1m 08.759s with Bottas on 1m 08.846s and Rosberg only managing a 1m 08.944s. Alonso was 4th followed by Ricciardo, Magnussen, Kvyat, Räikkönen, Hamilton and Hulkenberg.

Wow, no Mercedes on the front row for the first time this year and the

Williams' boys looking strong for the race up front, and the team's first front row lockout since Juan Pablo Montoya and Ralf Schumacher at the German Grand Prix at Hockenheim in 2003 and Massa's first pole since Brazil in 2008!

QUALIFYING RESULT (Top 10)

Q3	Car No.	Driver (Constructor)	Q1 Time	Q2 Time	Q3 Time	Grid Pos.
1	19	**Felipe Massa** **Williams**	**1:10.292**	**1:09.239**	**1:08.759**	1
2	77	Valtteri Bottas Williams	1:10.356	1:09.096	1:08.846	2
3	6	Nico Rosberg Mercedes	1:09.695	1:08.974	1:08.944	3
4	14	Fernando Alonso Ferrari	1:10.405	1:09.479	1:09.285	4
5	3	Daniel Ricciardo Red Bull	1:10.395	1:09.638	1:09.466	5
6	20	Kevin Magnussen McLaren	1:10.081	1:09.473	1:09.515	6
7	26	Daniil Kvyat Toro Rosso	1:09.678	1:09.490	1:09.619	7
8	7	Kimi Räikkönen Ferrari	1:10.285	1:09.657	1:10.795	8
9	44	Lewis Hamilton Mercedes	1:09.514	1.09.092	No time	9
10	27	Nico Hülkenberg Force India	1:10.389	1:09.624	No time	10

Sergio Pérez - 5 place grid penalty for causing a collision in the Canadian Grand Prix.
Romain Grosjean - starts from pit lane after a gearbox change.
Max Chilton - 3 place grid penalty for a collision at the Canadian Grand Prix.

THE RACE

From Pole, Massa led away at the start of the race. Rosberg made a better start than Bottas from 3rd but Bottas quickly regained the position back. At the end of the first lap it's Williams one and two. Hamilton had a brilliant start from 9th followed by a storming first lap, by the end of which he had jumped up to 4th place. "I had a rocket start," Hamilton said after the race. "It's something we've be working hard on all year and it was one of the best I've ever had. You can't ever plan what's going to happen but I managed to put the car in all the right places and climb to P4 by the end of the first lap." It was something to store in his memory banks that would serve him well later in the season.

At Red Bull's home race, Sebastian Vettel lost drive on lap 2. He carried on but was a lap down and also damaged his front wing, he later retired midway through the race.

Massa, Bottas, Rosberg and Hamilton kept station in close proximity until the first set of pit-stop between laps 13 and 16. Pérez was on a different tyre strategy and found himself in the lead after the frontrunners had pitted. Painfully slow in and out laps and traffic had dropped Massa down to 4th. Bottas having had a good pit-stop came out in 3rd behind the fast flying Rosberg. Pérez led until he too pitted at the end of lap 26.

The 4 Mercedes' powered cars were out in front in the same order until the next set of pit-stops on lap 40 and Alonso took over the lead for 5 laps until he stopped for his 2nd pit-stop. At the second set of pit-stops Hamilton leapfrogged Bottas and the order was now Rosberg, Hamilton, Bottas and Massa. The optimism of the Williams' team had now been broken and they knew their work was cut out to beat the Mercedes' duo. It was now between Hamilton and Rosberg, and although Hamilton honed in on Rosberg towards the end, he could not overtake.

Sergio Pérez again drove a good race with a different tyre strategy, taking the super soft compound only for the last laps and successfully challenging Kevin Magnussen for sixth place. Meanwhile, Alonso had closed in on Massa who was in 4th, but with the straight line speed of the Mercedes' engined Williams' was unable to pass. Alonso said, "I think that I can consider this to be my best race of the season, because finishing eighteen seconds off the Mercedes in a race without a Safety Car or any particular incidents, is a good result. It was impossible to keep Hamilton behind me and fifth place is really the best we could do today, because the first four cars were quicker and therefore deserved to finish ahead of us. We pushed hard all race without any problems, which means that little by little, we are improving."

Rosberg was delighted after his 3rd win of the season, "It wasn't the easiest of races - trying to manage certain things that were a bit on the limit on the car. But in the end I had a very, very fast car again, so it was fantastic to win today. It's great also to get a one-two here in Austria and it's great to come back here to Austria. I mean Austria for sure deserves a race. The fans have been amazing, the atmosphere has been spectacular this weekend, so thank you very much for that and yeah it's been awesome." Team mate Hamilton was also pretty satisfied with his race after starting from a lowly 9th. "We were managing the brakes a lot today, because I was in traffic for most of the race and it was the most important thing to bring the car home, so that was a real balancing act," he said. "But the strategy worked really well for me to get into second position, then I tried to start pushing Nico - but he didn't make any mistakes and I didn't have the chance to overtake."

The gap between Rosberg and Hamilton has now increased to 29 points in favour of the German and Rosberg seems to have the momentum after Hamilton's 4 race splurge.

AUSTRIAN GRAND PRIX 2014 RACE RESULT

Pos.	No.	Driver (Constructor)	Laps	Time	Grid	Points
1	6	**Nico Rosberg** **Mercedes**	71	**1:27:54.976**	3	25
2	44	Lewis Hamilton Mercedes	71	+1.932	9	18
3	77	Valtteri Bottas, Williams-Mercedes	71	+8.172	2	15
4	19	Felipe Massa Williams-Mercedes	71	+17.357	1	12
5	14	Fernando Alonso Ferrari	71	+18.553	4	10
6	11	Sergio Pérez Force India-Mercedes	71	+28.546	15	8
7	20	Kevin Magnussen McLaren-Mercedes	71	+32.031	6	6
8	3	Daniel Ricciardo Red Bull-Renault	71	+43.522	5	4
9	27	Nico Hülkenberg Force India-Mercedes	71	+44.137	10	2
10	7	Kimi Räikkönen Ferrari	71	+47.777	8	1

DRIVERS' CHAMPIONSHIP

Pos. Driver   Points

1 **Nico Rosberg**   **165**
2 Lewis Hamilton   136
3 Daniel Ricciardo   83
4 Fernando Alonso   79
5 Sebastian Vettel   60

CONSTRUCTORS' CHAMPIONSHIP

Pos.	Constructor	Points
1	**Mercedes**	**301**
2	Red Bull-Renault	143
3	Ferrari	98
4	Force India-Mercedes	87
5	Williams-Mercedes	85

THE BRITISH GRAND PRIX

SILVERSTONE

ROUND 9
SILVERSTONE CIRCUIT
BRITISH GRAND PRIX

ENG-LAND!

HAMILTON REGAINS THE HIGH GROUND AFTER QUALIFYING ERROR

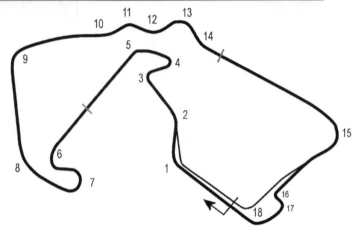

Date: 6 July 2014

Official Name: 2014 Formula 1 Santander British Grand Prix

Circuit: Silverstone Circuit, Silverstone, United Kingdom

Lap Length: 5.9 km (3.7 miles)

Lap Record: 1m 33.401s - Mark Webber (2013)

Distance: 52 laps, 306.7 km (190.6 miles)

QUALIFYING

It rained before qualifying but had subsided to a light drizzle as the drivers headed out for Q1. All the drivers were on the inters with the green sidewalls. Everyone was on track, except the Williams' team mates, anxious to set a lap time in case the rain increased. 5 minutes into the session and Lewis Hamilton laid down a marker time of 1m 43.676s in his Mercedes. Most of the rest of the drivers quickly posted times as more rain was reported to be on the way. However, as is commonplace at Silverstone, the track was also drying in places. The Williams finally came out with 9 minutes to go with first Massa going 5th. Then Bottas jumped him. The order at the top was Hamilton, Ricciardo, Rosberg, Vettel, Bottas and Massa. With 2 minutes everyone was on track on slicks, as the track continued to dry out and became much faster, and nine drivers had yet to set a quick enough time to qualify. Rosberg beat Hamilton's time to go top. Kvyat did a 1m 41.032s lap to go 2nd. Alonso spun in his Ferrari and Sutil went into a sand trap. The top 6 at the end were Rosberg, Kvyat, Hamilton, Bianchi, Hulkenberg and amazingly at his home Grand Prix, Chilton, to earn his first place in Q2 of the year. The 6 drivers out were Bottas, Massa, Alonso, Räikkönen, Ericsson and Kobayashi. Vettel was 16th and had just squeezed into Q2.

In Q2, the drivers were now back on the inters. 6 minutes in, Rosberg topped the session with a 1m 45.292s and then team mate Hamilton beat that with a 1m 44.639s. A minute later Vettel topped the times with a 1m 44.085s as the track dried. Hamilton pitted for slick tyres. 2 minutes later, Vettel had his time deleted by the officials because he ran wide at Copse. The track was now dry enough for slicks and the times came tumbling down. First, Gutierrez set a 1m 40.913s on slicks, then Vergne set a 1m 38.310s. Rosberg got down to a 1m 35.179s as the track continued to dry, with a response from Hamilton of a 1m 35s dead. So the top 10 in Q2 were Hamilton, Rosberg, Vettel, Button, Kvyat, Hulkenberg, Pérez, Kevin Magnussen, Vergne and Ricciardo. The 6 drivers eliminated were Grosjean, Bianchi, Chilton, Gutierrez, Pastor Maldonado and Sutil.

Everyone started on slicks in Q3. Kvyat posted the first time of 1m 40.707s. Pérez beat that with a 1m 40.457s. It was now raining lightly on some parts of the track. With 7 minutes to go Hamilton turned in a 1m 39.232s while Rosberg posted a 1m 39.426s. Pérez was 3rd ahead of Ricciardo, Kvyat, Vergne, Button, Hulkenberg, Magnussen and Vettel. 4 minutes remaining and everybody was in the pits preparing for their final run. As they set out, the track was very slippery, so the chances of the drivers improving their times were minimal. However, Vettel improved with a time of 1m 37.386s to take provisional pole. On his final run, Hamilton wasn't improving on his previous best time in the wet conditions on the first part of the lap and backed off on the Wellington Straight with Rosberg behind him. Rosberg carried on with his lap and found the second part of the circuit was now considerably drier than it had been earlier in the session. Rosberg grabbed pole with a 1m 35.766s. Button jumped to 3rd ahead of Hulkenberg and Magnussen. Hamilton wound up 6th, Pérez 7th. Hamilton's miscalculation had handed Rosberg the upper hand and he was clearly distraught.

QUALIFYING RESULT (Top 10)

Q3	Car No.	Driver (Constructor)	Q1 Time	Q2 Time	Q3 Time	Grid Pos.
1	6	**Nico Rosberg** **Mercedes**	**1:40.380**	**1:35.179**	**1:35.766**	1
2	1	Sebastian Vettel Red Bull	1:45.086	1:36.410	1:37.386	2
3	22	Jenson Button McLaren	1:44.425	1:36.579	1:38.200	3
4	27	Nico Hülkenberg Force India	1:41.271	1:37.112	1:38.329	4
5	20	Kevin Magnussen McLaren	1:42.507	1:37.370	1:38.417	5
6	44	Lewis Hamilton Mercedes	1:41.058	1:34.870	1:39.232	6
7	11	Sergio Pérez Force India	1:42.146	1:37.350	1:40.457	7
8	3	Daniel Ricciardo Red Bull	1:44.710	1:38.166	1:40.606	8
9	26	Daniil Kvyat Toro Rosso	1:41.032	1:36.813	1:40.707	9
10	25	Jean-Eric Vergne Toro Rosso	1:43.040	1:37.800	1:40.855	10

Max Chilton - 5 place grid penalty for gearbox change.

Esteban Gutiérrez - 10 place grid penalty for unsafe release at previous round and a 5 place grid penalty for gearbox change.

Pastor Maldonado - excluded from results for not having enough fuel to return to the pits.
Marcus Ericsson and Kamui Kobayashi - lap time outside 107% of Rosberg's fastest lap in Q1. They were given permission to start by race stewards.

THE RACE

Lights out and all the cars survived the inevitable bunch up at the first corner, but as the field careered down the Wellington Straight, Kimi Räikkönen went very wide coming out of Aintree. As he tried to rejoin the field along the straight, just before the footbridge, the car suddenly snapped right, sending the Ferrari into the barriers with some force. The Ferrari then bounced back onto the track in front of oncoming rear of the field, flailing debris and wheels in all directions. Massa took decisive evasive action but sent his Williams into a spin, catching the rear of the Ferrari and damaging his car and although he attempted to carry on he had to retire. A loose wheel from Räikkönen's car narrowly missed Chilton's head in the Marussia as the Ferrari came to a standstill on the other side of the track. The crash had looked serious and there was some concern over Räikkönen's condition, but he suffered only bruising, although he was certainly very shaken. "I had managed to get away well, making up enough ground to be fighting for 11th place," Räikkönen said. "At Turn 5, I went off the track and while trying to get back on, I must have hit a curb. I then lost control of the car and ended in the barriers. It's a real shame because yesterday, the feeling I had on track had improved and I was determined to do my utmost to bring home some points."

The race was stopped as the Marshall's cleared the extensive debris and was delayed by over an hour as they repaired the barrier that the Ferrari had hit, displacing it from its moorings. Mercedes' Niki Lauda criticised the delay saying that the chances of anyone else hitting the same dislodged guardrail were almost zero.

Rosberg took the lead again on the restart of the race, and Hamilton rampaged to 2nd by lap 4, looking as if he had something to prove after his error in qualifying. It appears we are in for another battle between the Mercedes' team mates. Hamilton protected his tyres for a few laps, with

Rosberg's lead stretching out to 5.7 seconds by lap 9, but then he began to haul Rosberg back. Hamilton now appeared to have the momentum. Hamilton was only 2.8 seconds behind by the time Rosberg made his first pit stop on lap 18. He reported "problems on the downshift" two laps later. Hamilton stayed out for a further six laps, with the intention of having a shorter stint at the end of the race in which he could attack his team-mate. He rejoined 5.9 seconds behind after a slow pit stop. But then Hamilton took a second out of his team mate on lap 27 and then a further two seconds next time around as Rosberg started to report up-shift problems. Rosberg was clearly in trouble and Hamilton took over the lead on lap 25 as Rosberg coasted to a stop, his first retirement of the season and the bad luck that Hamilton had suffered in Australia and Canada, was now being visited upon the German.

Bottas was now in second from Ricciardo. Red Bull had put Ricciardo and Vettel on the hard tyres for the restart. Then Ricciardo switched to the mediums on lap 15 and only made the one pit stop. Button was in 4th and crossed the finish line just 0.895 of a second behind the Australian. The latter's tyres were so worn out that he could not have kept Button behind for even one more lap. "Circuits with high-speed changes of direction aren't really our car's forte," Button said, "so I think we can go away from Silverstone feeling encouraged by what we achieved this weekend. Specifically, it was great to have such a good fight with Fernando, and it was encouraging to be able to pull away from him and Sebastian in the last stint. At the end, I crossed the line only 0.9s behind Daniel, if there'd been just one more lap, I think I could have made it past. I got so close to a podium finish - and I think it would've been so great for the fans to see Lewis and me up there together." Ricciardo, meanwhile was thrilled with his 3rd. "This is the best third place I've ever got," he said. "I'm not normally ecstatic with a third but I really am today, obviously to redeem myself from yesterday and also the fact that I don't think we had an awesome race car today, but we made it work. We used the cards that we had and played the game well, so I was really happy to make a one stop work. For the last two laps, I saw Jenson coming and thought I was probably going to be a bit vulnerable, but we held on. The one stop wasn't planned. We pitted quite early on the Prime because we were quite slow and it wasn't working, so we came in for the Option and, at one point, my engineer pretty much said alright, four laps to go on this tyre, then let's box."

Bottas was also delighted to be 2nd, his best ever finish. "We knew that this race could be good fun," said the Williams driver. "We knew that we had a quick car. Maybe it was a bit surprisingly quick today, but since the first stint the pace was good, since the first lap. I was able to go through the field quite well. Of course, sometimes it needed a bit of risk, because it's really important to get through quickly and not get stuck behind people, but I really managed to get well in position, where the pace of the car was. I'm just really, really happy with what we've been doing as a team. Again, the race pace shows we are really doing the right things and I'm very happy to be part of this. I said the pace seems OK, the tyres aren't getting any worse and let's try and stay out or at least think about keeping me out there and he said OK we'll look at our options. Then, a few laps later he said do you think you can go to the end, there's 15 or 20 laps to go, and I said, at the moment I think we can give it a crack. And so, yeah, we did and it paid off!"

One of the highlights of the race was the wheel to wheel duel between Alonso and Vettel. Both drivers raced on their limit, and both were complaining over the radio that the other was exceeding track limits. Eventually, after a thrilling few laps, Vettel, just inches away from Alonso, finally overtook him and then pulled away to finish 5th. "It felt very close with Fernando - maybe a bit too close!" said Vettel. "It got a bit silly when we both started to complain about the other going off track. I don't think the people care too much if the car is a little bit to the left or the right. I got the message that I should respect the limits and that he was complaining, so I was doing the same thing. I'm not sure who won the list keeping. I think twice it was maybe a bit too harsh into Turn 6, but it was good to get the move at the end. I expected to get third today, the pace was there but the strategy wasn't right. I'm looking forward to my home race in Germany, it's always special to race there."

Alonso said his car was only fast enough to finish sixth. "Today's race was very spectacular, certainly for us it was extremely hectic, first with Kimi's retirement and then with the penalty for being out of position at the start. Then there were also my duels with Button and Vettel. When Sebastian came up behind me, I was saving fuel and battery power and had a problem with the rear wing so I knew that sooner or later he would have overtaken me. I think both Red Bulls deserved to finish ahead of us, because they were quicker."

Hamilton was absolutely ecstatic with his 5th win of the season. "Winning in front of your home crowd is just the best feeling," said Hamilton who did donuts in his car for the 120,000 British crowd on the slow down lap and screamed 'Eng-land' over the radio. "We really do have the greatest fans here and thank you so much to everyone for your patience after yesterday. To see the support all around the track is just amazing. I said before that I'd never give up but it was a tough qualifying and I really needed to dig deep and come back positive this morning. A huge thank you to my family and all of the fans for pushing me on - I couldn't have done it without them. Today, I felt I earned it. From the start some good manoeuvres and I really felt that I had the pace on Nico. I really was hunting him down like never before. I really was happy with the balance that I managed to get, even though I didn't do the long run in P2. To say this is up there with all the greats, it's my home Grand Prix, it's my second win here and I'm very privileged to have even just had one, so I feel very humble to be up here today."

"I had a small issue in the installation lap but the car felt great in the beginning," he continued. "By lap 20, though, the gearbox started to become a serious problem and from then it got worse. I tried to get it into some safety settings, let Lewis through and just keep going until the end of the race. But there was nothing we could do so I had to stop the car. All I can do is accept that these things happen and work with the team to find out what went wrong."

Mercedes' technical boss Paddy Lowe said, "We decided to put the drivers on different tyre strategies, with Nico planning to run option/option/prime - and Lewis offset on the slower option/prime/option strategy, which could have given him a chance to challenge for the lead in the closing laps. It was shaping up that way until Nico's problems. It was a real blow to lose Nico's car. There was an early sign of a problem with a strange downshift, then it went away for 10 laps before recurring. We tried to change settings to remedy the situation but ultimately he lost drive and had to retire."

The rollercoaster ride between Rosberg and Hamilton continues on with Lewis now only 4 points behind Nico in the championship!

BRITISH GRAND PRIX 2014 RACE RESULT

Pos.	No.	Driver (Constructor)	Laps	Time	Grid	Points
1	44	**Lewis Hamilton** **Mercedes**	**52**	**2:26:52.094**	**6**	**25**
2	77	Valtteri Bottas Williams-Mercedes	52	+30.135	14	18
3	3	Daniel Ricciardo Red Bull-Renault	52	+46.495	8	15
4	22	Jenson Button McLaren-Mercedes	52	+47.390	3	12
5	1	Sebastian Vettel Red Bull-Renault	52	+53.864	2	10
6	14	Fernando Alonso Ferrari	52	+59.946	16	8
7	20	Kevin Magnussen McLaren-Mercedes	52	+1:02.563	5	6
8	27	Nico Hülkenberg Force India-Mercedes	52	+1:28.692	4	4
9	26	Daniil Kvyat Toro Rosso-Renault	52	+1:29.340	9	2
10	25	Jean-Éric Vergne Toro Rosso-Renault	51	+1 lap	10	1

DRIVERS' CHAMPIONSHIP

Pos.	Driver	Points
1	**Nico Rosberg**	**165**
2	Lewis Hamilton	161
3	Daniel Ricciardo	98
4	Fernando Alonso	87
5	Valtteri Bottas	73

CONSTRUCTORS' CHAMPIONSHIP

Pos.	Constructor	Points
1	**Mercedes**	**326**
2	Red Bull-Renault	168
3	Ferrari	106
4	Williams-Mercedes	103
5	Force India-Mercedes	91

THE GERMAN GRAND PRIX

HOCKENHEIM

ROUND 10
HOCKENHEIMRING
GERMAN GRAND PRIX

GERMANY RULES THE WORLD

WHILE HAMILTON STORMS TO 3RD FROM 20TH

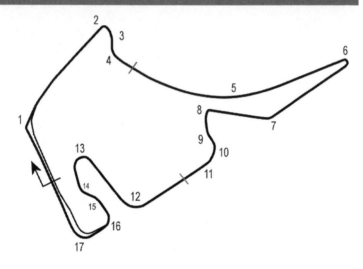

Date: 20 July 2014

Official Name: 2014 Formula 1 Großer Preis Santander von Deutschland

Circuit: Hockenheimring, Hockenheim, Germany

Lap Length: 4.6 km (2.8 miles)

Lap Record: 1m 13.780s - Kimi Räikkönen (2004)

Distance: 67 laps, 306.5 km (190.4 miles)

The 2014 German Grand Prix was the 61st time the race has been run as a round of the Formula One World Championship. The event was criticised for its poor fan turnout. Two weeks before the race, the FIA announced a ban on the Front and Rear Interconnected suspension system (FRIC), effective immediately. On Sunday, July 13th Germany had beaten Argentina 1-0 in the Football World Cup Final in Rio de Janeiro, Brazil. Nico got married to long-time girlfriend Vivian Sibold on Sunday. Can Germany rule in Germany?

QUALIFYING

In Q1 Massa put his Williams on top early on with a lap of 1m 19.389s, but Magnussen beats it with a 1m 19.379s. Ericsson was missing due to hydraulic problems. 6 minutes into the session Lewis Hamilton clocked a time of 1m 18.683s. Teammate Rosberg spun out on his first run. 4 minutes later Bottas topped the time sheets with a 1m 18.215s. Vettel was 5th and Ricciardo was 6th. With 8 minutes remaining Hamilton locked up and spun off at 130mph and crashed heavily into the tyre barriers at Turn 13. Q1 was red flagged. Hamilton was silent at first as his team radioed him to see if he was OK. Eventually, seemingly winded, he said, "I'm OK, ohh, something made the brakes fail." It appears his bad luck had returned.

9 minutes later the session was restarted. Rosberg hadn't set a time yet. There was 7 minutes and 21 seconds remaining in Q1. Rosberg was first out now on the supersoft tyres and set a decent time of 1m 17.631s. With 2 minutes left, Ricciardo was 2nd and Vettel was 3rd. The top 6 at the end were Rosberg, Ricciardo, Vettel, Bottas, Magnussen and Massa. The 6 drivers eliminated were Sutil, Bianchi, Maldonado, Kobayashi, Chilton and Ericsson. Mercedes posted on twitter that, "Lewis Hamilton is back from the medical centre. He's OK, but sore from the crash. We are working to diagnose the cause." Hamilton had had a right front brake failure and was 16th, which would have still put him into Q2 if the car hadn't been so damaged.

4 minutes into the session, Rosberg went quickest with a 1m 17.109s, with Bottas 2nd, Massa 3rd and Alonso 4th. 2 minutes later Vettel moved into 3rd and Magnussen into 4th. The top 10 at the end of Q2 were Rosberg, Bottas, Massa, Vettel, Magnussen, Ricciardo, Alonso, Hulkenberg, Kvyat and Pérez with Button, Räikkönen, Vergne, Gutierrez, Grosjean and Hamilton out.

In Q3, Rosberg posted an early time of 1m 16.540s. Next was Bottas with a 1m 17.057s followed by his Williams' team mate Massa with a 1m 17.306s. With 5 minutes to go, Vettel snatched 4th, with Magnussen 5th followed by Ricciardo, Alonso, Kvyat, Hulkenberg and Pérez. The drivers headed for the pits to prepare for one final run. On their final runs, with 3 minutes remaining, Pérez moved up to 6th. with seconds to go, Ricciardo took 3rd but promptly lost it to Massa. Then Magnussen went 4th. Rosberg was also out but couldn't better his earlier time. The top 10 were thus Rosberg, Bottas, Massa, Magnussen, Ricciardo, Vettel, Alonso, Kvyat, Hulkenberg and Pérez.

QUALIFYING RESULT (Top 10)

Q3	Car No.	Driver (Constructor)	Q1 Time	Q2 Time	Q3 Time	Grid Pos.
1	6	**Nico Rosberg Mercedes**	1:17.631	1:17.109	1:16.540	1
2	77	Valtteri Bottas Williams	1:18.215	1:17.353	1:16.759	2
3	19	Felipe Massa Williams	1:18.381	1:17.370	1:17.078	3
4	20	Kevin Magnussen McLaren	1:18.260	1:17.788	1:17.214	4
5	3	Daniel Ricciardo Red Bull	1:18.117	1:17.855	1:17.273	5
6	1	Sebastian Vettel Red Bull	1:18.194	1:17.646	1:17.577	6
7	14	Fernando Alonso Ferrari	1:18.389	1:17.866	1:17.649	7
8	26	Daniil Kvyat Toro Rosso	1:18.530	1:18.103	1:17.965	8
9	27	Nico Hülkenberg Force India	1:18.927	1:18.017	1:18.014	9
10	11	Sergio Pérez Force India	1:18.916	1:18.161	1:18.035	10

Esteban Gutiérrez - 3 place grid penalty as a result of an accident with Pastor Maldonado in the British Grand Prix.

Lewis Hamilton - 5 place grid penalty for a gearbox change.

Marcus Ericsson - failed to set a lap time in Q1 and also received a 10 second stop and go penalty because his team failed to cover and seal his car before curfew and therefore breached Parc Fermé regulations.

THE RACE

Off the line Rosberg took the lead from Bottas. The first lap was marred for the second race running and once again featured the unlucky Felipe Massa, when Kevin Magnussen collided with his Williams and sent him barrel rolling through the air. Massa, unhurt, was livid with Magnussen. "For me, he was too aggressive," Massa said. "He tried to brake, but when he tried, he touched me. When he saw that he was going to touch, he braked and that was a problem because I was already on the gas and he braked and I jumped. I was doing my line. If you are doing your line and you are in front, the guy behind needs to see and to brake. I couldn't see him. My line was not so tight, my line was a normal line. If I saw him, for sure, I would do whatever I can not to cause the accident, but it was impossible to see him there. He knew that there were two cars there." Magnussen, meanwhile, defended his position. "For sure if I had another place to go I wouldn't have had contact," he said. "I'm sorry about the situation, but I did my best and tried to avoid him, but I didn't really have anything to do. I wasn't really trying to do anything with Felipe so to have contact with him was very unfortunate."

Daniel Ricciardo, who had qualified in 5th, had to take avoidable action when Massa and Magnussen collided and dropped to 15th place. He charged back to finish 6th and crossed the line only 800th of a second behind Alonso's Ferrari. "That was awesome fun, one of my most enjoyable races I've had!" Ricciardo said. "I mean, not on the first lap, obviously, that was just the wrong place at the wrong time. I wasn't as worse off as Massa and hopefully he is okay. I was on the outside and the collision happened, I had to avoid it and went pretty far down the field, I don't know exactly how far back. From then on I just got on to the radio and said let's make an amazing recovery and make ourselves proud today. And I think we did that, we fought hard and we didn't leave anything on the table. These are the moments and battles that I personally thrive off and enjoy. Fernando is known to be a tough racer and I thought, who better to have a good fight with. I was on the Primes and he was on fresher Options and I gave it the best fight I could and, well, nearly!"

Rosberg was in a league of his own as he controlled the race and increased his lead over Bottas who remained pretty comfortable in 2nd until he had to fend off a fast charging Hamilton. Williams had put Bottas on a 2 stop strategy and he had to do the last 27 laps on the soft compound tyre. But all talk was about Hamilton's storming drive from 20th on the grid to achieve a extremely credible 3rd, after his crash in qualifying had required a gearbox change which meant he had a 5 place grid penalty on top of his lowly 16th position. Unperturbed, Lewis drove brilliantly as he carved his way through the field, which included some great battles and impressive overtakes along the way including one with former team mate Jenson Button. Hamilton made a late lunge on him and they touched from which Hamilton ended up with a damaged right front wing endplate. "It was very hard to get through the pack safely," he said. "I had a little bit of a collision with Jenson. I honestly thought he was opening the door to let me past, he's been a bit like that in the past, so my bad on judgment there. It's very hard to overtake at the end, they were so fast on the straights but I'm very happy I got some points today."

Hamilton started on the soft tyres and stormed up the placings and when the front runners, who had started on the supersofts pitted first, he moved into 2nd place on lap 16. After Hamilton pitted, Bottas reclaimed 2nd. Towards the end of the race, however Hamilton began to close in on Bottas, but Hamilton's supersoft tyres didn't have the legs and he didn't have the grip to get past Bottas. Alonso had fierce battles with both the Red Bulls but although he just stayed in front of Ricciardo, he couldn't resist the challenge of Vettel, who got 4th. "It was fun with Fernando today," Vettel said. "We started maybe where we left off in Silverstone! It was quite entertaining the first half of the race and at one point it was quite tight with both the Ferraris, but we managed to stay ahead. The second stop was a bit too close and Fernando was able to pass without too many difficulties, which put us on the back foot, but we decided to be a bit more aggressive towards the end and make sure we got the undercut and then we could put some gap between us, which was crucial for us as we were quite tight in terms of fuel towards the end of the race. I think that was the best we could get today." Alonso was pleased to finish 5th and Ricciardo had his usual huge grin after taking 6th place. Button was 8th. Magnussen and Pérez rounded out the top 10. Daniil Kvyat made a dramatic retirement when his Toro Rosso caught on fire when an ignition problem resulted in unburned fuel igniting in the exhausts.

Rosberg was over the moon with his home win plus he had got married in the run-up to the race and also Germany had won the World Cup against

Argentina in Brazil. "Wow, what a great day after so many great events for me this week!" he said. "I came here hoping for a win and it worked out perfectly. My Silver Arrow was so dominant, thanks to the team for this fantastic car. Before the race I was worried that without the FRIC system the gap in the race would be smaller. But we were again the quickest out there. I did a two stop strategy, which was difficult to manage at the end of the stints as the tyres were almost gone. I'm so happy for Mercedes, it was the first win for many, many years in Germany. Thanks for the support here at Hockenheim, the fans were amazing to me. Also at the start I saw a Mexican wave, which was great. Now I look forward to Hungary."

Bottas, who had achieved his second 2nd in 2 races and his 3rd podium in a row, was obviously overjoyed. "I am really happy with the way the race went today. As a team we have been unlucky not to have both drivers on the podium as we had the pace. To keep a Mercedes behind at the end of the race was promising, showing that it is possible, and the car is very strong. The engineers shared a lot of information with me about the tyres and where Hamilton was and that teamwork was the key to the good result."

The gap at the top of the championship, which swings one way then the other, has now increased to 24 points in Rosberg's favour, and Hamilton cannot afford to have too many more weekends as he did in Hockenheim.

GERMAN GRAND PRIX 2014 RACE RESULT

Pos.	No.	Driver (Constructor)	Laps	Time	Grid	Points
1	6	**Nico Rosberg Mercedes**	67	1:33:42.914	1	25
2	77	Valtteri Bottas Williams-Mercedes	67	+20.789	2	18
3	44	Lewis Hamilton Mercedes	67	+22.530	20	15
4	1	Sebastian Vettel Red Bull-Renault	67	+44.014	6	12
5	14	Fernando Alonso Ferrari	67	+52.467	7	10
6	3	Daniel Ricciardo Red Bull-Renault	67	+52.549	5	8
7	27	Nico Hülkenberg Force India-Mercedes	67	+1:04.178	9	6
8	22	Jenson Button McLaren-Mercedes	67	+1:24.711	11	4
9	20	Kevin Magnussen McLaren-Mercedes	66	+1 Lap	4	2
10	11	Sergio Pérez Force India-Mercedes	66	+1 Lap	10	1

DRIVERS' CHAMPIONSHIP

Pos.	Driver	Points
1	**Nico Rosberg**	**190**
2	Lewis Hamilton	176
3	Daniel Ricciardo	106
4	Fernando Alonso	97
5	Valtteri Bottas	91

CONSTRUCTORS' CHAMPIONSHIP

Pos.	Constructor	Points
1	**Mercedes**	**366**
2	Red Bull-Renault	188
3	Williams-Mercedes	121
4	Ferrari	116
5	Force India-Mercedes	98

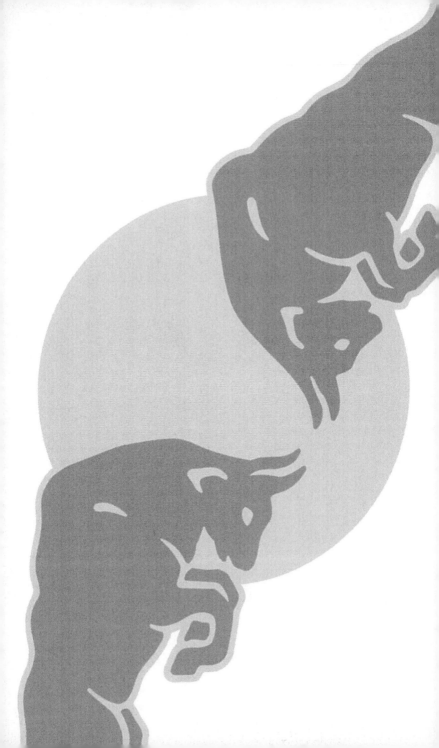

THE HUNGARIAN GRAND PRIX

HUNGARORING

ROUND 11
HUNGARORING
HUNGARIAN GRAND PRIX

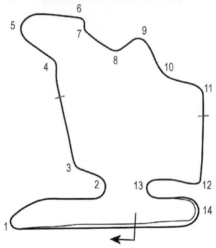

Date: 27 July 2014

Official Name: Formula 1 Pirelli Magyar Nagydíj 2014

Circuit: Hungaroring, Mogyoród, Hungary

Lap Length: 4.4 km (2.7 miles)

Lap Record: 1:19.071 - Michael Schumacher (2004)

Distance: 70 laps, 306.6 km (190.5 miles)

The race was only the 3rd Hungarian Grand Prix to be rain affected, after 2006 and 2011. Heavy rain soaked the track before the race, with all the drivers starting on inters before the track dried out later. Marussia changed the chassis of Max Chilton's car following electrical and balance problems that date back to the Austrian Grand Prix. Williams introduced a small wing section, aimed at increasing the amount of downforce and grip. Lotus brought new front wing endplates, which were designed to direct the airflow more efficiently.

QUALIFYING

5 minutes into Q1 and disaster once again struck Lewis Hamilton when he came into the pits with his Mercedes on fire. Meanwhile Bottas put his Williams on top with a 1m 25.690s with Ricciardo 2nd with a 1m 25.838s. 2 minutes later Gutierrez set a great time of 1m 25.709s to go 2nd while Rosberg took first with a 1m 25.353s and Vettel took his Red Bull to 2nd. Then Ricciardo went fastest with a 1:25.495 in the sister car. With Maldonado and Hamilton out, at least two of the usually slower drivers were guaranteed to make it to Q2. Rosberg took over at the top with a 1m 25.227s but with 2 minutes left, Vergne went quickest with a 1m 24.941s while his teammate Daniil Kvyat went 3rd behind Rosberg. In the closing seconds Bianchi grabbed 2nd place and thus relegated Räikkönen to 17th and outside the cut off after the team had decided not to send him out for a second run. The top 6 at the end of Q1 were Vergne, Rosberg, Kvyat, Ricciardo, Vettel and Bottas. The 6 drivers out were Räikkönen, Kobayashi, Max Chilton, Marcus Ericsson, Hamilton and Maldonado.

In Q2 everyone was on the softer compound tyres. 2 minutes into the session, Kvyat set the time to beat with a 1m 24.706s. Bottas was the first to beat it with a 1m 24.001s while his teammate Felipe Massa moved in behind him. A minute later, Rosberg clocked a 1m 23.310s while Alonso went 3rd. 2 minutes later Vettel went 2nd with his team mate Ricciardo in 3rd. A minute later, all the cars were in the pits and Rosberg, Vettel, Ricciardo and Pérez sat out the rest of the session in their respective garages. Massa went out for one more run and secured 5th. The top 6 ended up as being Rosberg, Vettel, Ricciardo, Bottas, Massa, Alonso, Button, Magnussen and Hulkenberg. The 6 out were Kvyat, Sutil, Pérez, Gutierrez, Grosjean and Bianchi.

Then it began to rain. They all went out on slicks to try and get in one good lap before the track got too wet. Rosberg spun off at Turn 1 and Magnussen crashed into the tyre wall at the same point and the red flags were out. The rain was increasing over some areas of the track. Q3 was stopped for 8 minutes while the marshals removed debris and repaired the barriers. With just under 10 minutes remaining Rosberg, Ricciardo and Bottas went out on slicks again and Rosberg set a 1m 26.488, but both Bottas and Ricciardo beat him. The track was beginning to dry and Alonso went 2nd. The drivers were all going for 3 fast laps in a row. Then with 5 minutes left Vettel took the provisional pole. But a minute later Rosberg set a 1m 23.236s to take over the provisional pole as the grip improved. Whoever was out there in the final seconds would have an advantage. The order was Rosberg, Vettel, Bottas. The provisional pole switched again when Vettel set a 1m 23.301s which Rosberg beat with a 1m 22.715s. Bottas was up to 3rd and Ricciardo 4th followed by Alonso, Massa, Button, Vergne, Hulkenberg and Magnussen.

QUALIFYING RESULT (Top 10)

Q3	Car No.	Driver (Constructor)	Q1 Time	Q2 Time	Q3 Time	Grid Pos.
1	6	**Nico Rosberg** **Mercedes**	**1:25.227**	**1:23.310**	**1:22.715**	1
2	1	Sebastian Vettel Red Bull	1:25.662	1:23.606	1:23.201	2
3	77	Valtteri Bottas Williams	1:25.690	1:23.776	1:23.354	3
4	3	Daniel Ricciardo Red Bull	1:25.495	1:23.676	1:23.391	4
5	14	Fernando Alonso Ferrari	1:26.087	1:24.249	1:23.909	5
6	19	Felipe Massa Williams	1:26.592	1:24.030	1:24.223	6
7	22	Jenson Button McLaren	1:26.612	1:24.502	1:24.294	7
8	25	Jean-Eric Vergne Toro Rosso	1:24.941	1:24.637	1:24.720	8
9	27	Nico Hülkenberg Force India	1:26.149	1:24.647	1:24.775	9
10	20	Kevin Magnussen McLaren	1:26.578	1:24.585	no time	PL

THE RACE

It is extremely difficult to pass in the Hungarian Grand Prix around its tight and twisting circuit. Somebody forgot to tell that to Daniel Ricciardo, however, as he pulled off an audacious pass on Lewis Hamilton and then sliced by Fernando Alonso and went on to score the second victory of his F1 career.

Hamilton and Magnussen started from the pit lane. Lewis was in a new car after the fire had ruined his car. Kevin started in a repaired McLaren after he had crashed in qualifying.

The race started on a wet track after it had rained before the race. Everyone started on inters, even though the rain had stopped. Pole sitter Rosberg took the lead ahead of Bottas, Vettel and Alonso. Ricciardo had made a bad start and had dropped to 6th from 4th. Meanwhile Hamilton spun off the track on the first lap and brushed the barrier, having started from the pit lane. But he quickly recovered and started to make up places from the back and was 13th when Ericsson put his Caterham into the barriers with some force and the safety car was immediately out. "I was just a bit too eager in the throttle," Ericsson said. "The back stepped out and I couldn't catch the car and that was it, I was in the wall. It was a pretty big shunt! I went to the medical centre straight after the crash and they told me it was about 20G, but physically I feel fine." Just as the Safety Car was about to pit, Grosjean crashed his Lotus almost exactly at the point where Ericsson had gone off. "The conditions on the circuit this afternoon were very tricky," he said, "and we couldn't get the best out of the tyres. We made the right call to move to slicks when the safety car came out - like most of the grid did - but I made a mistake when I was trying to keep the tyres warm. Unfortunately, I touched the white line and spun, and that was it."

The safety car really worked against the 4 top runners as they had already passed the pit entrance when it came out and had to do another lap before pitting. Everyone but Magnussen pitted to change tyres and all drivers changed to slicks except for Button, who is renowned for going the contradictory way to everyone else and stuck to the inters. The Safety Car finally came in at the end of lap 13. It was now Ricciardo, Magnussen, Massa, Rosberg, Vergne, Vettel and Alonso. The track was still fairly damp as drivers tip-toed around the circuit, and Button's decision to stay on the inters seemed a touch of genius as he took the lead on lap 14, only to be re-passed by Ricciardo the following lap as the track dried. Ricciardo then led for 9 laps until lap 23.

On lap 23, Pérez rounded Turn 14 just before the pit straight and put his left rear on the wet concrete and the car immediately snapped right and he was in the pit wall with the car strewn across the track. This prompted a second safety car and Ricciardo made a late but decisive move to pit for fresh rubber. "We can win this," he told his team as he exited the pit lane. That put Alonso into the lead, with Rosberg third and Hamilton fifth in a train of cars being held up by Toro Rosso's Jean-Eric Vergne, in second, when the race restarted on lap 27. Massa and Bottas were the only other drivers to pit. "I knew that the first Safety Car played into our hands," Ricciardo said. "We inherited the lead there, pitting for slicks and then we were looking alright. Then we got the second Safety Car and obviously we pitted again for another set of tyres but we obviously lost the lead. I wasn't really sure what was going to happen. We were staying out pretty long that stint and we were leading a fair chunk of the mid-race, but then I knew we weren't going to get to the end on that set of tyres. So we had to pit again and that put me back out of position. Then we knew we had to overtake to win the race." Rosberg pitted 5 laps later, fitting 'softs' and would have to make another stop. Meanwhile, Hamilton ignored the fact that overtaking doesn't often happen in Hungary to be 2nd on lap 34.

Meanwhile on lap 32, Vettel threw away his own chances while ahead of Hamilton. Hamilton noticed that Vettel was dipping his left rear onto the wet concrete kerb at turn 14 which Pérez had done similarly which had resulted in his heavy crash. On lap 32 he did it once again but this time he didn't get away with and, just as Pérez had done, headed for the pit wall. At the last second he corrected the car with a brilliant save but lost several places in the process.

Alonso and Hamilton pitted for a second time on laps 38 and 39 respectively, which was for the last time. Their stops meant Ricciardo was leading again until his final stop on lap 54 when he came out 4th, behind Alonso, Hamilton and Rosberg. But Ricciardo closed the gap on the leaders hand over fist, from 6.6 seconds behind Hamilton on lap 57 to be just behind him on lap 61. Alonso was on suffering on his degrading soft tyres, Hamilton was on newer medium tyres with Ricciardo and the fast charging Rosberg on relatively fresh softs. Alonso, now really struggling with grip, cut the chicane on lap 63, which Hamilton reported to his team, "Fernando gained an advantage," but it was Ricciardo that he needed to concentrate on, just behind him and with his significantly superior grip.

On a different strategy, Rosberg closed to within a couple of seconds of Hamilton. Lewis was then told by his team to let his team mate past as he was on a different tyre strategy but Hamilton ignored it because, although Nico had closed the gap, it had remained stable for some time and Hamilton would have had to slow down significantly to let him through. Rosberg complained on the radio, asking why Hamilton was not letting him past.

Hamilton, knowing he really needed to stay ahead of his main rival, refused, saying: "Tell him to get closer." Rosberg stopped on lap 56 for his final pit-stop.

Then Ricciardo joined the Hamilton club of disregarding the overtaking tradition when he took 2nd with a barnstorming move around the outside of Hamilton at Turn 2 on lap 67 and subsequently overtook Alonso's struggling Ferrari for the lead at the start of the next lap. "That's how you do it, ladies," he screamed on the radio which wasn't broadcast on the coverage. "I had the advantage of the fresher tyres," Ricciardo said, "but I knew they wouldn't make it easy. I attempted Lewis into Turn 2, I think the previous lap or maybe two before I eventually got him, but just locked up and went too wide. I had a second crack at it and I still locked up but I managed to just hang on and just had a bit more grip around the outside there, so that was that. And then, once I got close enough to Fernando, I knew I just had to go for it. Being in that sandwich there, Lewis was still I think in the DRS zone, basically I couldn't waste too much time and that's what I did and then once I got the lead I knew it was just a couple of laps to go."

Alonso managed to hold off Hamilton till the end, while Rosberg, after his final stop again closed in to the back of his team mate and was all over the back of the sister Mercedes. Again Hamilton was aggressive but fair in his defence and managed to stay ahead of Rosberg to cap an amazing race that he started in the pit lane and finished in 3rd at the end, with the bonus of gaining a few points over his team mate in the championship, albeit only 3 points. He had turned adversity into a pyrrhic victory and surely he would have won the race if it hadn't been for the fire.

Up front, Ricciardo took the chequered flag with 5 seconds back to Alonso, who had his best result of the season. "Winning this today, it honestly feels as good as the first," Ricciardo said. "It sank in a lot quicker this one, so crossing the line today I knew what was going on a bit more and it's like I could enjoy it immediately rather than it being delayed, it was awesome. To have to pass guys again to win the race, as I did in Canada, makes it a lot more satisfying, knowing that we did have a bit of a fight on our hands - you beauty! In this environment now I feel, I am a different driver and in a way a different person, a different sportsman than I was last year. I've got a lot more belief in myself and it's cool, I definitely feel like I belong here now and I've got confidence. Obviously, we've converted two races into wins this year so far and I think that confidence is showing. I've got some friends from Australia here this weekend, so the plan was to always have a few drinks tonight, so I think we've got an excuse to now!"

Alonso was only 600th of a second ahead of the attacking Hamilton with Rosberg a further half a second behind after giving up on attempting to pass his defensive team mate. "This podium means a lot to me and the whole team," Alonso said after the race, "because after so many difficult races, we managed to get the most out of everything, also taking a few risks, and second place seems like a win. To do 31 laps at the end on used soft tyres was a great challenge. At that point, the strategy suggested that if we had made a third stop, we could have finished fourth, but we decided to run to the flag instead."

Hamilton, however, is pretty unhappy about all the bad luck he has been having. "I was just pushing as hard as possible to get as high as I could," he said. "It was obviously damage limitation after what happened yesterday. I can't express the pain I feel when we have issues such as in the last couple of races. It's hard to swallow and difficult to come back the next day and get the right balance between not attacking too much, but pushing to the limit."

Rosberg was clearly downcast. "That was a disappointing afternoon," he said. "A few things didn't work out for me and it was a very up and down race. In the beginning it was all under control. Unfortunately the Safety Car cost me the lead, because I just missed the pit entry and then I couldn't pit. I also had some braking issues after the safety car went in and a difficult period of time with handling this, which cost me some positions. Then I was able to push a lot. I had a great last stint and at the end there was one chance to overtake Lewis in the last lap, but it didn't work out. So that is massively disappointing. We need to sit down and analyse internally what went wrong today. I'm still leading the championship, which is a positive thing, and I'll be ready to attack again after the summer break."

The top ten was rounded off by Massa, Räikkönen, Vettel, Bottas, Vergne and Button. The Hungarian Grand Prix was one of the best races of the season, with 5 different race leaders and a great finish and the 3 leading cars separated by less than a second with only a handful of laps remaining.

The Grand Prix circus now takes a summer break, with a gap of four weeks until the next Grand Prix, in Belgium, at the end of August.

HUNGARIAN GRAND PRIX 2014 RACE RESULT

Pos.	No.	Driver (Constructor)	Laps	Time	Grid	Points
1	3	**Daniel Ricciardo** **Red Bull-Renault**	70	1:53:05.058	4	25
2	14	Fernando Alonso Ferrari	70	+5.225	5	18
3	44	Lewis Hamilton Mercedes	70	+5.857	PL1	15
4	6	Nico Rosberg Mercedes	70	+6.361	1	12
5	19	Felipe Massa Williams-Mercedes	70	+29.841	6	10
6	7	Kimi Räikkönen Ferrari	70	+31.491	16	8
7	1	Sebastian Vettel Red Bull-Renault	70	+40.964	2	6
8	77	Valtteri Bottas Williams-Mercedes	70	+41.344	3	4
9	25	Jean-Eric Vergne Toro Rosso-Renault	70	+58.527	8	2
10	22	Jenson Button McLaren-Mercedes	70	+1:07.280	7	1

DRIVERS' CHAMPIONSHIP

Pos.	Driver	Points
1	**Nico Rosberg**	**202**
2	Lewis Hamilton	191
3	Daniel Ricciardo	131
4	Fernando Alonso	115
5	Valtteri Bottas	95

CONSTRUCTORS' CHAMPIONSHIP

Pos.	Constructor	Points
1	**Mercedes**	**393**
2	Red Bull-Renault	219
3	Ferrari	142
4	Williams-Mercedes	135
5	Force India-Mercedes	98

THE BELGIAN GRAND PRIX

SPA

ROUND 12
CIRCUIT DE SPA-FRANCORCHAMPS
BELGIAN GRAND PRIX

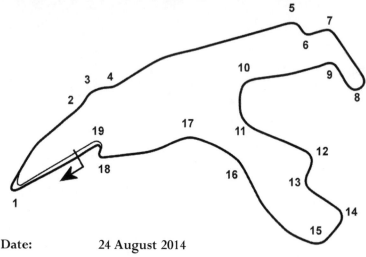

Date: 24 August 2014

Official Name: 2014 Formula 1 Shell Belgian Grand Prix

Circuit: Circuit de Spa-Francorchamps, Stavelot, Belgium

Lap Length: 7 km (4.4 miles)

Lap Record: 1m 47.263 s - Sebastian Vettel (2009)

Distance: 44 laps, 308.052 km (191.415 miles)

Tyre supplier Pirelli brought the medium primes and the soft options. There were two driver changes heading into the race. Having been in one of the two Caterham cars since the first race of the season in Australia, Kamui Kobayashi was replaced by 3 times winner of the Le Mans 24 hour endurance race, André Lotterer.

QUALIFYING

There had been significant heavy rain before Q1 started and although it stopped before the session began there was still a lot of standing water on the track. Most drivers started on the inters but some, including Bottas, had the extreme wets on. Bianchi set the first time of 2m 16.474s, some 25 seconds slower than a dry pace. Bottas then beat it with a 2m 10.750s. But the track was drying as the cars' tyres gradually cleared the standing water, but there was still plenty of spray around. 5 minutes in, Ricciardo clocked a 2m 10.642s and Hamilton dipped below the 2m 10s mark with a 2m 09.492s lap. 3 minutes later, Hamilton smashed his earlier time with a 2m 07.587s and his team mate moved behind him with a 2m 07.792s. Vettel was a long way behind Rosberg in 3rd, with a time of 2m 10.105s. With only a few moments left, Rosberg went quickest with a 2m 07.130s. At the end of the session the top 6 were Rosberg, Hamilton, Mass, Bottas, Vergne and Räikkönen. The 6 eliminated were Maldonado, Hulkenberg, Chilton, Gutierrez and Caterham newcomer André Lotterer and Ericsson.

In Q2 the drivers were still all on the inters as the track was still wet. Alonso set the early benchmark with a 2m 08.470s. Then with 8 minutes left, Rosberg set a 2m 08.108s. Sutil was 10th and on the bubble for getting into Q3. A minute later, Hamilton went from being out of the top 10 to the front with a 2m 07.089s. With 2 minutes left all the drivers were on track. With seconds to go Button was 11th while Vettel was 10th. Button then went 9th, pushing Vettel out, but the German responded to go 7th and Button was on the cusp. However, no one could go faster and he survived the cut. The top 10 were Hamilton, Rosberg, Alonso, Bottas, Räikkönen, Massa, Vettel, Magnussen, Ricciardo and Button. The 6 out were Kvyat, Vergne, Pérez, Sutil, Grosjean and Bianchi.

The sun was now out, although the track was still wet. Vettel was out first as the green light went on to signal the start of the session and went quickest, but Rosberg annihilated his time by over 2 seconds. Alonso was 3rd, Massa 4th and Hamilton 5th. Then Bottas went 4th, Ricciardo went

5th and Button was 6th, dropping Hamilton down the ranks. With 5 minutes to go, Hamilton took 2nd. 3 minutes later everyone was on track for their final runs. Vettel could not improve on his time. Rosberg then went even faster with a 2m 05.591s. Hamilton started his lap with 21 seconds to go but ended up just over 2 tenths shy of his team mate. After a series of bad qualifying sessions, Hamilton had at least stopped the rot and 2nd place on the grid is no bad thing with the electrifying starts that he has been making. Up front, Rosberg has again beaten the usually dominant qualifying record of Hamilton to grab his 8th pole of the season and the qualifying tally between the two team mates is now 8-4 in Rosberg's favour. But the two of them are way ahead of the field with a massive 2 second gap back to Vettel in 3rd. The race should be a breeze for the Mercedes' team, unless they trip over each other. The top 10 for the grid were Rosberg, Hamilton, Vettel, Alonso, Ricciardo, Bottas, Magnussen, Räikkönen, Massa and Button.

QUALIFYING RESULT (Top 10)

Q3	Car No.	Driver (Constructor)	Q1 Time	Q2 Time	Q3 Time	Grid Pos.
1	**6**	**Nico Rosberg** **Mercedes**	**2:07.130**	**2:06.723**	**2:05.591**	**1**
2	44	Lewis Hamilton Mercedes	2:07.280	2:06.609	2:05.819	2
3	1	Sebastian Vettel Red Bull	2:10.105	2:08.868	2:07.717	3
4	14	Fernando Alonso Ferrari	2:10.197	2:08.450	2:07.786	4
5	3	Daniel Ricciardo Red Bull	2:10.089	2:08.989	2:07.911	5
6	77	Valtteri Bottas Williams	2:09.250	2:08.451	2:08.049	6
7	20	Kevin Magnussen McLaren	2:11.081	2:08.901	2:08.679	7
8	7	Kimi Räikkönen Ferrari	2:09.885	2:08.646	2:08.780	8
9	19	Felipe Massa Williams	2:08.403	2:08.833	2:09.178	9
10	22	Jenson Button McLaren	2:10.529	2:09.272	2:09.776	10

THE RACE

Hamilton again made a better start off the line and took the lead, while Rosberg slotted in behind him. By the end of the first lap the two had already pulled a gap over 3rd placed Vettel. On the 2nd lap Rosberg was right on Hamilton's gearbox and as they approached Les Combes, Rosberg moved out of his team mates' slipstream and attempted to pass him on the outside. I say attempted, because it was pretty half hearted, as he dangled his front wing in Hamilton's line and there was really no way through. Then the inevitable happened as Rosberg clipped Hamilton's left rear tyre and damaged his own front wing. Hamilton carried on but was suddenly swerving all over the place as it became apparent that he had suffered a rear left puncture and he limped slowly to the pits having to travel the majority of the lap, which is one of the longest of the Grand Prix season. He eventually pitted for new tyres, but his race was effectively over and the team eventually withdrew his car.

Rosberg remained in front, although his pace had now been compromised by his damaged front wing and he made his first pit stop on lap 7 when he came in for new tyres and a new nose. Ricciardo, who had started fifth, passed Alonso and Vettel early on and took the lead on lap 8. 3 laps later he pitted, which left Bottas in the lead for a lap then Ricciardo was back in front. Rosberg climbed back to 2nd place after his first pit stop and was now charging fast. He pitted for new softs 10 laps from the end. Ricciardo made his final stop on lap 27 for a set of the mediums. Rosberg was 21 seconds behind but closed the gap at an amazing 3 seconds a lap.

Rosberg however never really got close to Ricciardo, finishing 3.383 seconds behind the Australian, who managed to eke out his tyres till the end to achieve his 3rd win of the season and the 2nd in a row to confirm him as the best driver of the year bar the Mercedes' pair. "You know everyone was saying we didn't really have a chance around here," Ricciardo said, "but I think we had some really good pace today and surprised ourselves. It feels a bit surreal, but another win is very cool, very cool. It was difficult staying out at the end of the race. When you're the leader as well, you always feel like you're the most vulnerable when it comes to a pit stop, but Simon my engineer came on the radio and said I think it's 11 laps left, can these tyres get to the end? And I said I think I can keep more or less this pace, and we were able to, and then on the last lap I found a couple more tenths, so I was having a bit of fun then!"

With all the controversy up front, it was easy to forget there were other drivers in the race, with Bottas getting his 4th podium in 5 races with 3rd place. "Obviously, yesterday, the weather played a role in the qualifying," he said, "and we knew that in the dry we would have better pace than in the wet, so we were really hopeful for today. I have to say that we are little bit surprised by the pace of Red Bull and Mercedes. They were quite a bit far away. Of course our race was a bit compromised after the poor start. I was quite a long time stuck behind some other cars and couldn't really go at the pace we had. But yeah, had some good overtakes. We had good pit stops and good strategy by the team and that allowed us to come up a few places and again to be on the podium."

Kimi Räikkönen, who battled with Bottas among other drivers, achieved a credible 4th in his Ferrari. "We had decided to tackle this race more aggressively, making an early stop to get ahead of the cars that had yet to pit and that meant I was able to stay with the leaders for much of the race," he said. "When Bottas in the Williams began to close on me, I knew I didn't have the speed to defend on the straight and with a few laps to go, he managed to pass me. In general, I'm happy with how this weekend ended. We knew it would not be easy on this circuit, but we did our utmost and for the first time, we managed to have a clean race without any problems. The car has improved and today the pace was good."

There were some really close encounters between Räikkönen, Bottas, Alonso, Vettel, Button and Magnussen. Vettel and Alonso came to blows on the final lap. "Towards the end of the race was good," said Vettel who was finally 5th. "I was in a rush to get through, because the laps were going down and obviously Alonso and Magnussen didn't have fresh tyres, so Jenson and I caught them fairly quickly. In the end it was good not to lose a position compared to when we decided to pit, which was probably a little bit late, but in the end we maintained the position. The battle was fairly interesting, it was a bit all over the place with people pushing each other off on the track, but we raced hard, although sometimes maybe a bit too hard!"

Magnussen was 6th, but he was penalised and eventually demoted to 12th after forcing Alonso off the track. "Despite being penalised after the race, I have to say I enjoyed the weekend," he said. "I had great fun out there this afternoon - I was involved in exciting racing on an awesome circuit. It was a tough challenge, because everyone around me had slightly fresher tyres than I did, and they're all great drivers. They're not the easiest guys to keep behind. So I just tried my best to defend my position as well as I could." His team mate, Button finished in 6th place.

Alonso finished in 8th after his race was compromised by a 5 second stop and go penalty after, with less than 15 seconds to go before the warm up lap, his mechanics were still trying to start his car. "Today my race started on the back foot as the car did not fire up and we had to use another battery," he said. "It's a shame because we had a strong pace all weekend and, starting fourth, we could have finished on the podium. With a penalty to take and on a circuit where top speed is our weak point, we knew we didn't stand much of a chance, but all the same we did our best. Unfortunately, towards the end there was some rather questionable driving and after my front wing was damaged in a coming together with Vettel, the important thing was to get to the chequered flag. I know the Stewards acted on what happened, but I don't think it's that important when you are fighting for sixth and seventh places."

But all talk was about the flashpoint between the Mercedes' duo with Hamilton absolutely furious over his team mates actions. "It looked quite clear to me but we just had a meeting about it and he basically said he did it on purpose," Hamilton said. "He said he did it on purpose, he said he could have avoided it. He said 'I did it to prove a point', he basically said 'I did it to prove a point'. And you don't have to just rely on me, go and ask Toto , Paddy and all those guys who are not happy with him as well. I was gobsmacked when I was listening to the meeting. You need to ask him what point he was trying to make." Rosberg attempted to defend his actions and gave his view of the controversial clash. "That was a tough race," he said. "We had the pace to win today but the incident cost us a top result, so I'm really disappointed because for the team it was a bad day. As drivers, we are here to entertain and to show the fans a good time, so our duels are always on the limit. I regret that Lewis and myself touched, but I see it as a racing incident - just as the stewards did. I was quicker down the straight and went to the outside as the inside line was blocked. I gave it a go and, after we touched, I realized that my front wing was damaged and thought that was it. In the next second I saw that Lewis also had a problem, which was very unfortunate for him and for the team. We sat down quickly after the race but there will be some more meetings to be held in order to avoid races like today."

Mercedes' bosses Toto Wolff and Niki Lauda were also angry at Rosberg and had blamed him for finishing Hamilton's race. "Nico felt he needed to hold his line," Wolff said countering Hamilton's account of their meeting. "He needed to make a point, and for Lewis, it was clearly not him who needed to be aware of Nico. He didn't give in. He thought it was for Lewis to leave him space, and that Lewis didn't leave him space. So they agreed to disagree in a very heated discussion amongst ourselves, but it wasn't deliberately crashing. That is nonsense. It was deliberately taking into account that if Lewis moves or would open then it could end up in a crash. What we saw there was that Nico was not prepared to take the exit, and that caused the collision. That is not something we want to happen."

There was some criticism of the way that Mercedes' was handling their drivers especially from ex Formula 1 team owner, Eddie Jordan, now working as a pundit for the BBC, who suggested the team was now in disarray and didn't know what they were doing. Toto Wolff said that Rosberg would be internally disciplined which probably means a monetary fine.

BELGIAN GRAND PRIX 2014 RACE RESULT

Pos.	No.	Driver (Constructor)	Laps	Time	Grid	Points
1	3	**Daniel Ricciardo Red Bull-Renault**	44	**1:24:36.556**	5	25
2	6	Nico Rosberg Mercedes	44	+3.383	1	18
3	77	Valtteri Bottas Williams-Mercedes	44	+28.032	6	15
4	7	Kimi Räikkönen Ferrari	44	+36.815	8	12
5	1	Sebastian Vettel Red Bull-Renault	44	+52.196	3	10
6	22	Jenson Button McLaren-Mercedes	44	+54.580	10	8
7	14	Fernando Alonso Ferrari	44	+1:01.162	4	6
8	11	Sergio Pérez Force India-Mercedes	44	+1:04.293	13	4
9	26	Daniil Kvyat Toro Rosso-Renault	44	+1:05.347	11	2
10	27	Nico Hülkenberg Force India-Mercedes	44	+1:05.697	18	1

Kevin Magnussen originally finished sixth but had 20 seconds added to his race time for forcing Fernando Alonso off track.

DRIVERS' CHAMPIONSHIP

Pos.	Driver	Points
1	**Nico Rosberg**	**220**
2	Lewis Hamilton	191
3	Daniel Ricciardo	156
4	Fernando Alonso	121
5	Valtteri Bottas	110

CONSTRUCTORS' CHAMPIONSHIP

Pos.	Constructor	Points
1	**Mercedes**	**411**
2	Red Bull-Renault	254
3	Ferrari	160
4	Williams-Mercedes	150
5	McLaren-Mercedes	105

THE ITALIAN GRAND PRIX

MONZA

ROUND 13
AUTODROMO NAZIONALE MONZA
ITALIAN GRAND PRIX

THE PRESSURE IS ON!
ROSBERG ERROR HANDS HAMILTON VICTORY

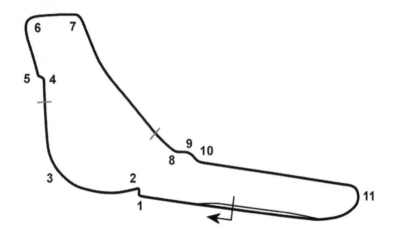

Date: 7 September 2014

Official Name: Formula 1 Gran Premio d'Italia 2014

Circuit : Autodromo Nazionale Monza, Monza, Italy

Lap Length: 5.8 km (3.6 miles)

Lap Record: 1m 21.046s - Rubens Barrichello (2004)

Distance: 53 laps, 306.7 km (190.6 miles)

THE RETURN OF THE SILVER ARROWS

All talk was what would happen if the 2 Mercedes' drivers clashed again on track. Hamilton was now on the back foot with 29 points between him and Rosberg in Rosberg's favour. For the 3rd consecutive year, Pirelli brought its two hardest tyre compounds to the Italian Grand Prix, with the orange-banded hard compound tyre being the harder prime tyre, and the white-banded medium compound tyre being the softer option. The Parabolica had been slightly altered for the race with a new run off tarmac area.

QUALIFYING

5 minutes into Q1, Rosberg, who had had gearbox problems, which had now been rectified, turned in a 1m 25.862s, which team mate Hamilton beat with a 1m 25.710, and then Massa beat them both with a 1m 25.607s. The times were now tumbling on the dry conditions and 10 minutes into the session, Rosberg clocked a 1m 25.493s which Massa improved on with a 1m 25.528s, bettered by Hamilton with a 1m 25.363s. 3 minutes to go and the top 6 were Hamilton, Rosberg, Massa, Bottas, Button and Magnussen. With the drivers now on the softer options, Vergne set a great time to go 5th while team mate Kvyat was 6th. Top 10 were Hamilton, Rosberg, Massa, Bottas, Vergne, Kvyat, Button, Magnussen, Hulkenberg and Alonso. The 6 out were Maldonado, Grosjean, Kobayashi, Bianchi, Chilton and Ericsson.

It wasn't until 6 minutes into Q2 that the frontrunners came out and Rosberg led the pack with a 1m 24.482s with Bottas behind with a 1m 24.882s. Hamilton was outside of the top 10, 9 minutes in, but then topped the timesheets with a 1m 25.560. In the last minute all 16 drivers were on the track but Rosberg couldn't wrestle first away from Hamilton. The top 10 in Q2 were Hamilton, Rosberg, Bottas, Massa, Alonso, Button, Vettel , Pérez, Ricciardo and Magnussen with the 6 drivers out being Kvyat, Räikkönen, Vergne, Hulkenberg, Sutil and Gutierrez.

Again Q3 was going to be a fight for pole between Rosberg and Hamilton. 4 minutes in and all the drivers were on track with Rosberg fastest on a 1m 24.552s with Bottas 2nd with a 1m 24.697s. Half way through, Hamilton moved to the top with a 1m 24.109s. Bottas was now demoted to 3rd ahead of Massa, Button, Vettel, Alonso, Magnussen, Ricciardo and Pérez.

With 4 minutes to go everyone went out for their final runs and although

Rosberg improved on his time he couldn't beat Hamilton. Bottas was still 3rd and Massa 4th, but Magnussen had now moved to 5th ahead of Button, Alonso, Vettel, Ricciardo and Pérez. Hamilton had achieved his first pole since the Spanish Grand Prix in May which was also the last time he had out qualified his team mate.

QUALIFYING RESULT (Top 10)

Q3	Car No.	Driver (Constructor)	Q1 Time	Q2 Time	Q3 Time	Grid Pos.
1	44	**Lewis Hamilton Mercedes**	**1:25.363**	**1:24.560**	**1:24.109**	1
2	6	Nico Rosberg Mercedes	1:25.493	1:24.600	1:24.383	2
3	77	Valtteri Bottas Williams	1:26.012	1:24.858	1:24.697	3
4	19	Felipe Massa Williams	1:25.528	1:25.046	1:24.865	4
5	20	Kevin Magnussen McLaren	1:26.337	1:25.973	1:25.314	5
6	22	Jenson Button McLaren	1:26.328	1:25.630	1:25.379	6
7	14	Fernando Alonso Ferrari	1:26.514	1:25.525	1:25.430	7
8	1	Sebastian Vettel Red Bull	1:26.631	1:25.769	1:25.436	8
9	3	Daniel Ricciardo Red Bull	1:26.721	1:25.946	1:25.709	9
10	11	Sergio Pérez Force India	1:26.569	1:25.863	1:25.944	10

Daniil Kvyat - 10 place grid penalty for using his 6th engine of the season.

THE RACE

With Hamilton and Rosberg on the front row the big worry was that they would clash again going into the first corner, a tight chicane after the main straight, but all fears were quickly dispelled when Hamilton had a problem off the line and dropped back to 4th before the first corner. "At the start there's a button that you press which engages the launch sequence," he said, "and for the formation lap it didn't work. I thought 'no problem, I'll just put it on for the race' and then when I got to the grid, I put it on and again it didn't work. It's very, very strange, I've never really had that happen before. There was a different sequence of lights that were on, that weren't on ever before. Anyway, I tried to pull away as fast as possible. The RPM was all over the place and fortunately I managed to not lose too many places."

Rosberg led away ahead of the fast starting rookie Magnussen and Massa. Meanwhile Bottas had lost places at the start and was down in 10th, due to the fact that he was directly behind the slow starting Hamilton. Massa passed Magnussen on lap 5 and Hamilton did likewise at the first of the Lesmo corners. Rosberg was feeling the pressure from the fast charging duo of Massa and Hamilton, who sets the fastest lap and on lap 9 the pressure got to him as he locked up in the braking zone at the first chicane and surprisingly takes to the escape road, losing a lot of time but retaining the lead. He now leads by only 2 seconds. Hamilton was soon challenging Massa for 2nd and finally got past him on lap 10 with a fine pass out of the chicane and was now chasing down his team mate and the nervous tension was again notched a peg or two upwards as Hamilton reeled him in.

On the same lap, the fast charging Bottas was making up for his bad start and passes Räikkönen for 9th while Vettel closes in on Magnussen in 4th. 4 laps later Bottas passes Pérez down the main straight for 8th. Meanwhile up front Rosberg's lead is down to 1.5 seconds. On lap 16 Bottas passes Alonso on the main straight for 7th as he continues to cut through the field in the fast Williams and on lap 18 passes Button on the main straight for sixth place. A lap later Vettel pits and switches to the primes. On lap 21 Bottas passes Magnussen at the first chicane to take 4th. Rosberg's lead is now down to 1.2 seconds and radios an annoyed message to tell his team not to keep informing him of the gap to Lewis. On lap 24 Massa pits from 3rd and rejoins in 5th. Mercedes tells Hamilton that it's Hammer Time.

Lap 25 and Rosberg pits, as does Bottas. A lap later Hamilton pits from the lead and rejoins directly behind his team mate, as Rosberg is told that he needs to watch his fuel consumption. Hamilton sets the fastest lap. Rosberg is really hot under the collar now and he makes the same mistake as he did earlier at the same point on the circuit, on lap 24, and again takes to the escape road at the chicane. This time he isn't so lucky, as Hamilton takes over the lead, which he never relinquishes and wins the Italian Grand Prix by over 3 seconds for his 6th win of the year. On the podium he said, "What a great crowd we have here. This is amazing to see. The whole finish line straight is completely filled with fans. You guys make this race, so thank you so much for the support." Rosberg was clearly saddened by the events and his errors. "Lewis was quicker this weekend, so he deserved the win," he said. "That for sure is very disappointing for me. I had a lock up in Turn 1 and I decided to go straight to avoid a flat spotted tyre. That cost me the lead. But he was very quick behind me, so I had to push all the time. Definitely very disappointing from that point of view. But then at the end of the day, also, first of all it's a great day for the team, because after the recent difficulties it's the first one-two for the team in a long time. And so that's back to where we need to be, so that's awesome. And then for me, of course I'm disappointed now right afterwards but in the end of it, still second place, still a lot of points, so it's not a complete disaster."

Massa was overjoyed with 3rd after some bad luck had plagued him this season. "It's a great day for us," he said. "It was a great race, a great start. Also the pace was very good. So, not enough to fight with Mercedes but I think we had a very good pace, a very good car. The team did a perfect job. I'm really, really happy to be on the podium today. We missed a little bit during the season to be on the podium, but so it's special to be on the podium here in front of these amazing people. Also, a very positive result for us that we passed Ferrari here as well, which is very important for us, very good for us. It's amazing to see how Williams were last year and we are fighting with big teams. Definitely it's really good for the whole team and we will keep fighting until the last race and I hope really we can get this third place in the constructors' championship. It would be fantastic for the whole team. I'm so happy to be on the podium here in this amazing place that I really love."

His team mate Bottas would have been on that podium but for his poor getaway. "Compared to the grip I had available in the tyres I think we were a bit aggressive with the clutch," he said. "The start for the formation lap, when we always do the final checks was compromised because Lewis had a slow getaway, so that maybe hurt a little bit. Definitely the tyres were not in the optimum window and maybe for that condition we were a bit too aggressive, I had a poor start but the same thing continued after Turn 2 - just wheel spinning after Turn 2. After the poor start the position I was in the chicane was a bit lucky, I couldn't accelerate at the maximum rate. That really compromised the race for me. It's a pity because today I came into the race with the mentality that this was the best chance of the season to fight for the win, so fourth is not really that satisfying."

Ricciardo was happy with his 5th. He passed a handful of higher powered engined cars in Räikkönen, Pérez, Magnussen, Button and his Red Bull team mate Vettel. "The strategy helped today," he said. "It kept the tyres fresh enough to go those extra few laps at the end. I saw the cars in front of me pit and the pace was still good enough, so seeing that we didn't have great pace when we were out of position, then we thought we would try something different and that's why we went long, which helped towards the end of the race. I was more comfortable with the prime tyre and was able to do some good moves, which kept me smiling. The start wasn't ideal, it's one of the longest runs up to Turn 1 here from the start line and it's not a place where you want to have a bad one, but I dropped the clutch and didn't get the traction, so we will have to look at that, but we kept a cool head and picked our way back through the field. I think fifth, even with a good start, was the best we could do."

Red Bull's Sporting Director Christian Horner said of their strategy, "I think fifth and sixth was the absolute optimum today. We picked two different strategies, an aggressive one with Sebastian to undercut the McLaren, which worked and gave him track position but unfortunately made his tyres marginal at the end of the race. With Daniel we took the opposite approach as he was running in clear air. We ran him long in the first stint with a shorter second stint and then his passing moves to come back through the field were truly impressive and obviously with Sebastian struggling with tyre degradation due to the length of the stint, it became inevitable that the two were going to swap positions. But fifth and sixth place, at a circuit dominated by Mercedes-powered cars, is damage limitation achieved." Vettel was once again beaten by Ricciardo. "I think that was the most we could do today," Vettel said. "On the primes we weren't able to look after the tyres as well as we wanted to. The target is to get back to the front, at the moment the gap is quite big but we will have to work hard to close it again. We have had some difficulties this year, but they can only make us stronger if we learn from them. In terms of strategy we wanted to get the McLarens so we went aggressive with the early stop, but the tyres started going off at the end and all in all that was what we could do today."

It was a bad day for Ferrari at their home Grand Prix with Alonso retiring with a mechanical problem, amazingly for the first time since 2009. "After a long run of trouble-free races, it's a real shame I had to retire just here in Monza, in front of all our fans," he said. "I would have liked to have put on a very different race for them. In the first stint we were competitive, but when you find yourself in a group of cars where everyone is using DRS, overtaking becomes nearly impossible. After the pit stop, I found myself at the back of a train of cars and at that point we changed the strategy, deciding to drop back from the group to conserve the tyres and try and attack at the end of the race. But then came the problem with the ERS system. It's never nice for the team to have a reliability problem, because the guys work night and day to give us the best car possible. What happened doesn't change my will to win and in order to try and have that happen soon, we will continue to work as hard as we can, always giving our all."

ITALIAN GRAND PRIX 2014 RACE RESULT

Pos.	No.	Driver (Constructor)	Laps	Time	Grid	Points
1	44	**Lewis Hamilton** **Mercedes**	53	1:19:10.236	1	25
2	6	Nico Rosberg Mercedes	53	+3.175	2	18
3	19	Felipe Massa Williams-Mercedes	53	+25.026	4	15
4	77	Valtteri Bottas Williams-Mercedes	53	+40.786	3	12
5	3	Daniel Ricciardo Red Bull-Renault	53	+50.309	9	10
6	1	Sebastian Vettel Red Bull-Renault	53	+59.965	8	8
7	11	Sergio Pérez Force India-Mercedes	53	+1:02.518	10	6
8	22	Jenson Button McLaren-Mercedes	53	+1:03.063	6	4
9	7	Kimi Räikkönen Ferrari	53	+1:03.535	11	2
10	20	Kevin Magnussen McLaren-Mercedes	53	+1:06.171	5	1

Kevin Magnussen - 5 seconds added to race time for forcing Valtteri Bottas off the track.

Marcus Ericsson - started from pit lane for infringing yellow flag during FP3.

Esteban Gutiérrez - 5 seconds added to race time for causing an avoidable collision with Romain Grosjean.

DRIVERS' CHAMPIONSHIP

Pos.	Driver	Points
1	**Nico Rosberg**	**238**
2	Lewis Hamilton	216
3	Daniel Ricciardo	166
4	Valtteri Bottas	122
5	Fernando Alonso	121

CONSTRUCTORS' CHAMPIONSHIP

Pos.	Constructor	Points
1	**Mercedes**	**454**
2	Red Bull-Renault	272
3	Williams-Mercedes	177
4	Ferrari	162
5	McLaren-Mercedes	110

THE SINGAPORE GRAND PRIX

MARINA BAY

ROUND 14
SINGAPORE INTERNATIONAL CIRCUIT
SINGAPORE GRAND PRIX

SINGAPORE SLING

ROSBERG LEFT HIGH AND DRY WITH ELECTRICAL PROBLEMS

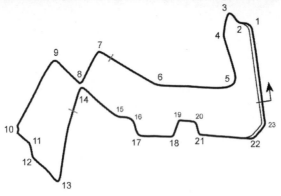

Date: Sunday, 21 September 2014

Official Name: 2014 Formula One Singapore Airlines Singapore Grand Prix

Circuit: Singapore International Circuit, Marina Bay, Singapore

Lap Length: 5.06 km (3.15 miles)

Lap Record: 1:48.574 – Sebastian Vettel (2013)

Distance: 60 laps, 303.9 km (188.9 miles)

Scheduled Distance: 61 laps, 309 km (192 miles)

As in the 2012, Pirelli brought its yellow-banded soft compound tyre as the harder prime tyre and the red-banded supersoft compound tyre as the softer option tyre, different to last year when the medium and supersoft were used. Going into the race, Rosberg lead in the Drivers' Championship, was down to 22 points. While in the Constructors' Championship, Mercedes were leading by a massive 182 points over Red Bull. In the weeks leading up to the race, the FIA announced plans to introduce a ban on certain pit to car communications, with a particular emphasis on banning driver coaching under Article 20.1 of the sporting regulations, which state that a driver must drive the car alone and unaided.

QUALIFYING

In the early stages of Q1 Rosberg made a slight error and went straight on at Turn 8, but he saved his car from spinning, as with the confined nature of the Singapore track, the walls can be unforgiving. Bottas set the time to beat with a 1m 48.743s. 6 minutes in and Rosberg moves into second with a 1m 48.775s. A minute later, after being impressive in Free Practice, Alonso, topped the time sheet with a 1m 48.203 and team mate Räikkönen went 2nd with a 1m 48.583s. A couple of minutes later Hamilton beats the two of them with a 1m 47.847s. Gutierrez, on the super softs went into 2nd with a 1m 4.970 s with 7 minutes left. Ricciardo stole first place while team mate Vettel was blocked by a slower car. Hulkenberg went faster with a 1m 47.370s. Then it was Räikkönen's turn to go fastest with a 1m 46.685s. The top 10 at the end of Q1 were Räikkönen, Alonso, Hamilton, Button, Bottas, Rosberg, Hulkenberg, Vergne, Vettel and Ricciardo. The six drivers eliminated were Sutil, Maldonado, Bianchi, Kobayashi, Chilton and Ericsson.

Q2 started with everyone on the supersofts and 1 minute in, Massa turned a 1m 47.535s. Then Räikkönen went fastest with a 1m 46.359s, beaten by his Ferrari team mate Alonso with a 1m 46.328s. Hamilton then put in a 1m 46.287s to top and the order behind him was Alonso, Räikkönen, Ricciardo, Rosberg and Vettel. On the final runs and with less than 2 minutes remaining, Massa took 4th with Bottas 8th. At the very end Rosberg set a quick time of 1m 45.825s. The top 10 were Rosberg, Hamilton, Alonso, Räikkönen, Massa, Ricciardo, Vettel, Bottas, Magnussen and Kvyat with Button, Vergne, Hulkenberg, Gutierrez, Pérez, and Grosjean out.

Massa went first in Q3 with a 1m 46.007s with Ricciardo and Räikkönen behind. Hamilton was 6th and Rosberg 7th, setting times on used tyres. With 5 minutes left the order was Massa, Ricciardo, Alonso, Räikkönen, Bottas, Hamilton, Rosberg, Vettel, Kvyat and Magnussen. On their final runs of Q3, Räikkönen had no power and had to pull off the track. Ricciardo grabbed the provisional pole with a 1m 45.854s, then Rosberg took it back with a 1m 48.688s, and finally Hamilton did a 1m 45.681s to grab pole. The final top 10 were Hamilton, Rosberg, Ricciardo, Vettel, Alonso, Massa, Räikkönen, Bottas, Magnussen and Kvyat.

QUALIFYING RESULT (Top 10)

Q3	Car No.	Driver (Constructor)	Q1 Time	Q2 Time	Q3 Time	Grid Pos.
1	44	**Lewis Hamilton** **Mercedes**	**1:46.921**	**1:46.287**	**1:45.681**	1
2	6	Nico Rosberg Mercedes	1:47.244	1:45.825	1:45.688	2
3	3	Daniel Ricciardo Red Bull	1:47.488	1:46.493	1:45.854	3
4	1	Sebastian Vettel Red Bull	1:47.476	1:46.586	1:45.902	4
5	14	Fernando Alonso Ferrari	1:46.889	1:46.328	1:45.907	5
6	19	Felipe Massa Williams	1:47.615	1:46.472	1:46.000	6
7	7	Kimi Räikkönen Ferrari	1:46.685	1:46.359	1:46.170	7
8	77	Valtteri Bottas Williams	1:47.196	1:46.622	1:46.187	8
9	20	Kevin Magnussen McLaren	1:47.976	1:46.700	1:46.250	9
10	26	Daniil Kvyat Toro Rosso	1:47.656	1:46.926	1:47.362	10

THE RACE

As the cars set off on the formation lap, Rosberg's car was stood still on the grid, while he frantically pressed various buttons and scrolled through various menus on his steering wheel, but to no avail. His mechanics finally pushed his car into his pit box and he had to begin the race from there. "The problems with my steering wheel began in the garage even before the race," he said, "and it was a difficult moment when I couldn't pull away from the grid - the car didn't get out of neutral. When I left the pit-lane, I was only able to change gear - there was no radio, no DRS and reduced Hybrid power. We were hoping that the systems might come back to life, like the radio did, and that we could change the situation. But after we changed the wheel another time, we had to retire the car. It was a tough day for me and unfortunately another reliability problem for the team."

Rosberg left a grid box sized hole for Vettel and Alonso to exploit and they duly obliged. As Hamilton disappeared up the road, Alonso, slid wide in the first corner as he passed Vettel, but then handed the place back. But on lap 31 fate opened the door for someone other than Hamilton to win, when Pérez crashed into Sutil and left debris strewn across the track and out came the safety car and changed many of the driver's strategy. Hamilton, on the super softs had to make one more stop. While behind him Vettel, Ricciardo and Alonso, were on the harder soft tyres, and decided not to stop again. At the restart Hamilton rocketed away to try to build a lead that would enable him to pit and still come out leading, but it was a tall order. "It was all running pretty comfortably until the safety car came out, which gave me some problems," he said. "I was driving hard to build the gap but then the tyres started dropping off and I wasn't sure what to do - keep pushing or back off to look after them. So we pitted straight away and I came out behind Seb." Hamilton needed a cushion of about 26 seconds but his tyres were degrading and with 10 laps to go he pitted with a lead of 25.2 seconds and came out just behind Vettel. "But I knew they were on a two-stop strategy and that his tyres were old," Hamilton said. "I went for it down the back straight - the gap was pretty small and maybe I could have chosen another point on the circuit. But I luckily squeezed through and made it stick." Hamilton soon passed the Red Bull driver. "As Lewis touched on, the overtaking manoeuvre, I wasn't quite sure what he was doing," he said. "I thought that I gave him all the space to pass me on the inside for the next corner but it seemed like he couldn't wait to get back in the lead. It was quite tight but I saw him, obviously, so I had to back-off and let him through. There was no point fighting him at that stage because

I didn't have the tyres to match him." Vettel stayed in second, leading a close three way battle with Ricciardo and Alonso. "I had a good start, got past Daniel and then I think we had a decent race," Vettel said. "We played a little bit with strategy and then the safety car came in the worst possible moment for us. So we tried to obviously stay out with the last set of tyres and make them work, which was very, very much borderline. I had a lot of pressure from Daniel and also from Fernando behind, but very happy obviously to make it P2."

Ricciardo was supported by a hoard of Australian fans. "We were really close to the Mercedes in qualifying and we expected the race pace to be a bit faster today to be honest," he said. "We weren't quick enough in the first stint and we had a few other issues going on, with brakes and some power issues that were coming and going, but in terms of points we still got a good handful to take away from here. It actually feels a bit like a home race here. Singapore to Perth is like Melbourne to Perth, so for West Australians it's not too far."

Alonso, in fourth, was disappointed with his start, which probably cost him the podium. "With hindsight, it's easy to ask oneself how things would have gone if I hadn't made a mistake at the start and the safety car hadn't come out when it did," Alonso said, "but overall I'm pleased with this weekend, because we were competitive and were able to fight with the front runners. Sometimes, a safety car can help but I think that today on this front, we were a bit unlucky, because at that moment, we were trying to make sure of second place and our strategy was good. We didn't have much of an alternative, because if we had stayed out, the probability was that the stop for the softs would have cost us more places. Even if in the end, I wasn't able to get past, the fact we were competitive right to the finish confirms we have made a step forward. Now, in Suzuka, a real circuit, we will have a clearer picture of where we are."

Massa who had started in 6th, ended up 5th. "We changed the strategy from a three-stop to a two-stop after the long safety car period," he said, "and the final stint was pushing the tyre to the absolute limit but I managed to make it work. The grip levels were very low in the final few laps but I had a big enough gap to sixth place to ease the car home. Given the nature of the track, fifth was probably the best position we could have hoped for this weekend." While team mate, Bottas, dropped to 11th from 6th in the last two laps with his tyres finally giving up the ghost, and giving him no grip. "After the safety car, we moved to a two-stop strategy and in the end the tyres just weren't able to hold on," he said. "In the final lap I had a big lock up in the rear tyres when I was defending and after that I had no grip and cars could easily sweep past. "I also had an issue with the power steering in the final stint and this made it harder to keep the tyres alive as I lost a lot of feeling in the car. If I hadn't had this issue then I might have been able to go until the end."

Lewis Hamilton blasted into the lead of the world championship by dominating the Singapore Grand Prix while his Mercedes team mate, Nico Rosberg, who had led the points, retired with a wiring loom problem. Hamilton now has 241 points to Rosberg's 238.

"I was dreaming it last night but you never really think it's going to happen," Hamilton said after winning his 7th race of the season. "I just want to say a huge thanks to my team. What they've done this year is absolutely incredible and to be able to arrive here knowing that we have a car we can fight with, and just the feeling I had through the race. I couldn't do it without them. Thank you guys." He had reversed his fortunes and now led the championship by a slender margin of 3 points.

SINGAPORE GRAND PRIX 2014 RACE RESULT

Pos.	No.	Driver (Constructor)	Laps	Time	Grid	Points
1	44	**Lewis Hamilton Mercedes**	60	**2:00:04.795**	1	25
2	1	Sebastian Vettel Red Bull-Renault	60	+13.534	4	18
3	3	Daniel Ricciardo Red Bull-Renault	60	+14.273	3	15
4	14	Fernando Alonso Ferrari	60	+15.389	5	12
5	19	Felipe Massa Williams-Mercedes	60	+42.161	6	10
6	25	Jean-Éric Vergne Toro Rosso-Renault	60	+56.801	12	8
7	11	Sergio Pérez Force India-Mercedes	60	+59.038	15	6
8	7	Kimi Räikkönen Ferrari	60	+1:00.641	7	4
9	27	Nico Hülkenberg Force India-Mercedes	60	+1:01.661	13	2
10	20	Kevin Magnussen McLaren-Mercedes	60	+1:02.230	9	1

Jean-Éric Vergne - 5 seconds added to his race time for exceeding track limits.

Nico Rosberg - starts from pit lane due to electronic problems at the start of the formation lap.

The power unit on Kamui Kobayashi's car failed during the formation lap and he failed to make it to the starting grid.

DRIVERS' CHAMPIONSHIP

Pos.	Driver	Points
1	**Lewis Hamilton**	**241**
2	Nico Rosberg	238
3	Daniel Ricciardo	181
4	Fernando Alonso	133
5	Sebastian Vettel	124

CONSTRUCTORS' CHAMPIONSHIP

Pos.	Constructor	Points
1	**Mercedes**	**479**
2	Red Bull-Renault	305
3	Williams-Mercedes	187
4	Ferrari	178
5	Force India-Mercedes	117

THE JAPANESE GRAND PRIX

SUZUKA

ROUND 15
SUZUKA CIRCUIT
JAPANESE GRAND PRIX

HAMILTON TYPHOONS PAST ROSBERG

BUT ALL THOUGHTS ARE FOR JULES BIANCHI

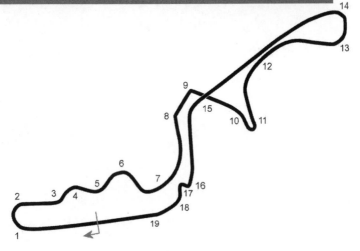

Date: 5 October 2014

Official Name: 2014 Formula 1 Japanese Grand Prix

Circuit: Suzuka Circuit, Suzuka, Japan

Lap Length: 5.8 km (3.6 miles)

Lap Record: 1:31.540 - Kimi Räikkönen (2005)

Distance: 44 laps, 255.5 km (158.8 miles)

Scheduled Distance: 53 laps, 307.8 km (191.2 miles)

Typhoon Phanfone, classified as a category one storm, was forecasted to make landfall over the eastern Japanese coast on the Sunday of the Grand Prix, accompanied by heavy rain and winds of up to 240 km/h. Although the predicted course of the storm was expected to miss Suzuka, the rain from the northern edge of the storm was expected to drench the circuit with steadily increasing heavy rain.

All the gossip, before qualifying, centres around a rumour that Vettel is about to leave Red Bull, to join Ferrari. Red Bull boss, Christian Horner is confident that Vettel will stay. Later, the paddock is awash with speculation after Vettel's move was confirmed in a press release after Vettel had texted Horner to ask if he could see him in his room. 'I knew it wasn't room service,' said Horner. Alonso's seat is the most likely for Vettel to take. But where will Alonso go? There was talk that he was hoping that Mercedes' contract negotiations with Lewis Hamilton would break down and that a vacancy at the Silver Arrows would suddenly open up but all indications are that the Hamilton/Mercedes relationship is set to continue beyond the end of the current contract which ends at the end of 2015. Alonso appeared to be gambling on the relationship breaking down. So, what are his choices now that that seems unlikely. Take a year off, move to McLaren or stay at Ferrari even though Vettel has announced his decision? If Alonso goes to McLaren, rather than taking a year out of the sport, he is likely to replace Jenson Button, possibly ending the 2009 World Champion's 15 year career. McLaren sources have indicated privately that Alonso would be granted No 1 status and paired with a youthful No 2. Red Bull immediately announced that 20 year old Russian Daniil Kvyat would be Vettel's replacement. Ferrari will confirm Vettel as their driver in the next few weeks.

QUALIFYING

In Q1 Rosberg set the early mark at 1m 33.671s with Bottas in 2nd place with a 1m 34.301s. Hamilton then took control after clocking a 1m 33.611s. 8 minutes in, Massa is 4th, Alonso is 5th with Magnussen, Button, Vettel and Ricciardo behind. And apart from a couple of movements that was pretty much how it remained and the top 10 at the end of Q1 Hamilton, Rosberg, Bottas, Massa, Alonso, Magnussen, Räikkönen, Hulkenberg, Button and Vergne with the bottom 6 being Maldonado, Grosjean, Ericsson, Bianchi, Kobayashi and Chilton.

Everyone was on the softer medium tyres for Q2. Sutil set the first time of

1m 36.656s beaten by Pérez with a 1m 35.089s. Then Bottas did a 1m 33.801s beaten by Rosberg with a 1m 32.950s. Hamilton went 2nd with a 1m 32.982s. 8 minutes to go, Ricciardo was right on the cusp with Vettel just ahead in 9th and a minute later Ricciardo was 12th and Vettel was 13th and in some danger, but managed to squeeze in on their last laps. On the final runs the Mercedes' duo decided to sit it out, feeling safe, and they were right. The top 10 at the end were Rosberg, Hamilton, Bottas, Massa, Alonso, Magnussen, Ricciardo, Button, Räikkönen and Vettel. The 6 drivers eliminated were Vergne, Pérez, Kvyat, Hulkenberg, Sutil and Gutierrez.

4 minutes into Q3 and alone on the track, Bottas clocked a lap time of 1m 33.329 with Massa behind on a 1m 33.527s. A minute later Rosberg was in front with a 1m 32.629s. Hamilton could not beat him with a 1m 32.946. After the first runs, behind the Mercedes, the order was Bottas in 3rd, Massa in 4th, Alonso in 5th, Magnussen in 6th, Ricciardo in 7th, Button in 8th, Vettel in 9th, and Räikkönen, who hadn't gone out, in 10th. Rosberg improved his time to a 1m 32.506 on his final run. Seconds later, Hamilton, locked up and although he improved to a 1m 32.703s, he couldn't better Rosberg. Bottas stayed in 3rd followed by Massa, Alonso, Ricciardo, Magnussen, Button, Vettel and Räikkönen.

QUALIFYING RESULT (Top 10)

Q3	Car No.	Driver (Constructor)	Q1 Time	Q2 Time	Q3 Time	Grid Pos.
1	6	**Nico Rosberg** **Mercedes**	**1:33.671**	**1:32.950**	**1:32.506**	1
2	44	Lewis Hamilton Mercedes	1:33.611	1:32.982	1:32.703	2
3	77	Valtteri Bottas Williams	1:34.301	1:33.443	1:33.128	3
4	19	Felipe Massa Williams	1:34.483	1:33.551	1:33.527	4
5	14	Fernando Alonso Ferrari	1:34.497	1:33.675	1:33.740	5
6	3	Daniel Ricciardo Red Bull	1:35.593	1:34.466	1:34.075	6
7	20	Kevin Magnussen McLaren	1:34.930	1:34.229	1:34.242	7
8	22	Jenson Button McLaren	1:35.150	1:34.648	1:34.317	8
9	1	Sebastian Vettel Red Bull	1:35.517	1:34.784	1:34.432	9
10	7	Kimi Räikkönen Ferrari	1:34.984	1:34.771	1:34.548	10

Pastor Maldonado and Jean-Éric Vergne - 10 place grid penalties for exceeding their quota of five engine components for the season.

THE RACE

It was a very dark day in Suzuka, in more ways than one. The heavy rain predicted for Sunday transpired. There was talk of holding the race in the morning to avoid the worst of the rain, but organiser's dismissed it as they wouldn't have been able to inform fans early enough for them to attend and were worried about a low turnout. More likely, race ticket refunds and TV slots were more important to them, because they could have taken such a decision even before the race weekend had begun, due to the predicted storm. It turned out to be a bad decision. The rain meant that the race had to be started behind the safety car, but after only 2 laps the race was red flagged, when it was obvious that the track was far too wet for racing. All cars unusually lined-up in the pit lane. The rain began to ease up when it seemed more certain that the race would be abandoned. 20 minutes after the red flag, the race again began behind the safety car. Alonso retired due to his car turning itself off just after the restart.

On lap 9, the safety car pitted and the green flags were out. Button followed the safety car in to pits for intermediates and found himself in 3rd after the other drivers gradually followed his lead. Rosberg was leading until lap 12 and he pitted to switch to the inters. Hamilton then led for 2 laps and then did the same. Rosberg kept his lead until lap 28. Hamilton was faster and passed him at the start of lap 29, with Rosberg struggling with oversteer. "Fairly straightforward, really," Hamilton said. "I had a lot more pace than Nico. This is not a very easy circuit to follow but fortunately I was able to get quite close and particularly in the last corner. I think perhaps he had a small oversteer moment out of the last corner and I didn't. Obviously the DRS enabled me to get alongside. I was fairly confident with the balance of the car so I put it there and stuck it out. And after that it was really about trying to... you know, the whole approach changed after that because I was attacking, attacking and after that, I kind of took different lines and managed it differently. But it felt very reminiscent of a time years and years ago, in 2008, and it was a great feeling in that respect."

A lap later the rain was visibly getting heavier. The track was becoming treacherous and Massa screamed on the radio for the race to be stopped. Then on lap 41 disaster struck, a situation that reminded us of how long ago it was that a driver lost their life on the circuits of the world, Ayrton Senna in 1994 in the San Marino Grand Prix. Sutil crashed his Sauber at Turn 7. Sutil's car was well away from the track but a recovery tractor had entered the circuit limits to remove his car. One lap later, Bianchi spun his Marussia at the same corner and his car careered towards the tractor, narrowly missing a marshal, but slamming into the tractor and going under it, with Bianchi's helmet hitting the underside, and the engine air intake sparking flames as it collided with the recovery vehicle. "What happened to Jules was the same thing that happened to me," a clearly distraught Sutil said. "The rain was increasing and daylight was going down. I was following Jules and I spun, so I ended up in the wall. I stood up and left the car, so the marshals tried to remove my car. One lap later Jules lost the car."

It was reported that Bianchi was unconscious immediately after the crash, following his failure to respond to a radio call from Marussia and the marshals that had attended the scene. He was taken by ambulance to the Mie University Hospital under police escort as the FIA later reported that the medical helicopter was unable to fly due to the precarious weather conditions, although it took off a short time afterwards. According to Bianchi's father he then underwent an operation to reduce severe bruising to his head. The FIA subsequently released a statement that CT scans have shown Bianchi suffered a 'severe head injury' in the crash, and he would be transferred to intensive care following surgery. Bianchi's family later reported that he had a diffuse axonal injury, which is a common traumatic brain injury in vehicle accidents involving high deceleration.

Out of respect for the injured Jules Bianchi, on the podium, the champagne stayed on ice and Hamilton, Rosberg and Vettel didn't celebrate - a spectacle that reminds us of bygone days, that we hoped would never happen again. "Our first thoughts go to Jules," said Hamilton who had just won his 30th Grand Prix. "It overshadows everything else when one of our colleagues is injured and we are praying for him."

"My thoughts are with our colleague Jules and his family and team mates," Rosberg said, "and we are hoping for some positive news."

"Everything that happened with the racing on track is secondary today," Vettel said. "One of us is in a bad shape. Jules had a bad accident and we hope to have some very good news, very soon. Not knowing what's going on feels terrible, I think all the drivers really feel with him, as we know how difficult and slippery it was today, we hope for the very best."

"When the race started the conditions were fine," Button said, "and I came straight into the pits to get intermediate tyres. There's a fine line between not being able to see and the tyres not being the right tyres. There is more spray than standing water, so I think it was safe conditions. I think the FIA did a really good job at controlling the situation. They are listening to the drivers - we want to go racing, but we want to do it in safe conditions. It's the spray that makes it dangerous, not the standing water, but I think they did a great job today."

But there are still questions of why the race hadn't been stopped when Sutil went off. Ex Formula 1 driver and Mercedes' boss, Niki Lauda said: "Motor racing is dangerous. We get used to it if nothing happens and then we are suddenly all surprised. But we always have to be aware that motor racing is very dangerous. This accident was the coming together of various difficult things. One car goes off, the truck goes out, and then the next car goes off. This was very unfortunate. In the end the rain was not the real issue of the race. There were safety cars put in and the race was run safe more or less to the end. So it could have been run to the end without the accident, so the darkness I don't think was an issue. The lesson learned is that in the difficult conditions of today, in the rain, that it could have been done differently because of the rain and the chance to go off was certainly bigger."

All our thoughts are now with Jules Bianchi who is critical but stable in a Japanese Hospital!

JAPANESE GRAND PRIX 2014 RACE RESULT

Pos.	No.	Driver (Constructor)	Laps	Time	Grid	Points
1	44	**Lewis Hamilton** **Mercedes**	44	1:51:43.021	2	25
2	6	Nico Rosberg Mercedes	44	+9.180	1	18
3	1	Sebastian Vettel Red Bull-Renault	44	+29.122	9	15
4	3	Daniel Ricciardo Red Bull-Renault	44	+38.818	6	12
5	22	Jenson Button McLaren-Mercedes	44	+1:07.550	8	10
6	77	Valtteri Bottas Williams-Mercedes	44	+1:53.773	3	8
7	19	Felipe Massa Williams-Mercedes	44	+1:55.126	4	6
8	27	Nico Hülkenberg Force India-Mercedes	44	+1:55.948	13	4
9	25	Jean-Eric Vergne Toro Rosso-Renault	44	+2:07.638	20	2
10	11	Sergio Pérez Force India-Mercedes	43	+1 Lap	11	1

Pastor Maldonado - 20 seconds added to his race time for pit lane speeding.

DRIVERS' CHAMPIONSHIP

Pos. Driver   Points

1 **Lewis Hamilton**   **266**
2 Nico Rosberg   256
3 Daniel Ricciardo   193
4 Sebastian Vettel   139
5 Fernando Alonso   133

CONSTRUCTORS' CHAMPIONSHIP

Pos.	Constructor	Points
1	**Mercedes**	**522**
2	Red Bull-Renault	332
3	Williams-Mercedes	201
4	Ferrari	178
5	Force India-Mercedes	122

THE RUSSIAN GRAND PRIX

SOCHI

ROUND 16
SOCHI AUTODROM
RUSSIAN GRAND PRIX

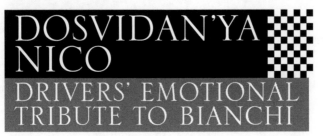

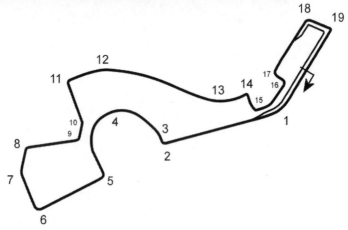

Date: 12 October 2014

Official Name: 2014 Formula 1 Russian Grand Prix

Circuit: Sochi Autodrom, Sochi, Krasnodar Krai, Russia - Semi-permanent racing facility

Lap Length: 5.9 km (3.6 miles)

Lap Record: Set at this Grand Prix, 1:40.896 - Valtteri Bottas (2014)

Distance: 53 laps, 310.2 km (192.8 miles)

After Jules Bianchi's tragic accident at the Japanese Grand Prix, the FIA announced that they planned to introduce a mandatory speed limiter to cars, that can be remotely activated from Race Control in the event of a yellow flag, restricting the driver to a speed limit of 100 km/h (62 mph) following reports that Bianchi had been travelling at 212 km/h (132 mph) when he lost control of his car. The system will be tested at the next race, the United States Grand Prix. Bianchi, meanwhile, remains stable but critical. Marussia entered only one car, driven by Max Chilton, leaving the grid with 21 cars. Marussia brought Bianchi's car to the race and left it in the pit box as a sign of respect to the driver.

The 2014 Russian Grand Prix was held at the Sochi Autodrom, a brand new circuit built around the site of the 2014 Winter Olympics in the city of Sochi in Krasnodar Krai, Russia. It was the first time that the Russian Grand Prix has been held in a century, and the first ever time that the Russian Grand Prix has been run as a round of the Formula One World Championship, which began in 1950.

Following the shooting down of Malaysia Flight 17 over eastern Ukraine in July, there were allegations that the Russian's were involved in the incident. There were calls from the British Conservative Party for Formula One to abandon the race as part of sanctions placed on the Russian government, as the race was funded by them. The race, however, went ahead. Both Vladimir Putin and Dmitry Kozak were in attendance, with Putin presenting the race winner's trophy.

QUALIFYING

In Q1, the Mercedes' drivers set the early pace with Rosberg on a 1m 39.292s and Hamilton on a 1m 40.061s. Hamilton improved on that with a 1m 39.282s with 12 minutes left and Rosberg bettered that with a 1m 39.076s a minute later only for Hamilton to dip below the 1m 39s mark for the first time over the weekend. Massa was the shock elimination, as he struggled with a fuel pressure issue that left him short of power. "Basically I had no power," he said, "and it looked like there was a problem with the fuel pressure, we were not getting enough fuel into the engine. I'm very disappointed because the car is really competitive here, but now I have to focus for the race. I can go back to one of my old engines if necessary, so that's not an issue, but today's result is massively disappointing." His team mate, Bottas, was the fastest driver through the speed trap but was still a second short of Hamilton's fastest time. The top 10 were Hamilton, Rosberg, Bottas, Button, Magnussen, Kvyat, Räikkönen, Alonso, Hulkenberg and Vergne. The 5 drivers out of Q1 were Ericsson, Massa, Kobayashi, Maldonado and Chilton. Unusually all drivers contested Q1 on the softer medium tyre.

In Q2, the Mercedes' boys began where they left off in Q1, with Rosberg putting in a lightning time of 1m 38.979s but then surprisingly, Bottas beat it. Hamilton then shaved a massive 6 tenths off of his time. Vettel and Ricciardo were struggling with a lack of grip and Vettel was in the drop zone and eventually could only manage 11th and was out of Q2. The top 10 ended up as Hamilton, Rosberg, Bottas, Magnussen, Kvyat, Button, Ricciardo, Alonso, Räikkönenand Vergne with the 6 out were Vettel, Hulkenberg, Pérez, Gutierrez, Sutil and Grosjean.

Q3 began and Ricciardo set the top early time of 1m 40.076s. But order was resumed when Rosberg topped the time sheets from Bottas, Button, Alonso, Kvyat, Hamilton, Ricciardo, Vergne, Räikkönen and Magnussen. Then Ricciardo went 4th, recovering from his early tyre grip problems. 4 minutes to go and Hamilton was on a flier and grabbed provisional pole with a 1m 38.467s. Rosberg was also on a quick lap but lost 3 tenths in the final sector and was in 2nd. Hamilton then threw in a 1m 38.513s just to be certain and achieved his 7th pole of the season. However, Bottas was on his way to beating that time when he slid wide in the final corner, when on the absolute limit and lost 7 tenths of a second. Russian driver, Daniil Kvyat, achieved his best ever qualifying at his home Grand Prix in a very popular 5th place. The top 10 on the grid were Hamilton, Rosberg, Bottas, Button, Kvyat, Magnussen, Ricciardo, Alonso, Räikkönen and Vergne.

QUALIFYING RESULT (Top 10)

Q3	Car No.	Driver (Constructor)	Q1 Time	Q2 Time	Q3 Time	Grid Pos.
1	44	**Lewis Hamilton Mercedes**	**1:38.759**	**1:38.338**	**1:38.513**	1
2	6	Nico Rosberg Mercedes	1:39.076	1:38.606	1:38.713	2
3	77	Valtteri Bottas Williams	1:39.125	1:38.971	1:38.920	3
4	22	Jenson Button McLaren	1:39.560	1:39.381	1:39.12	4
5	26	Daniil Kvyat Toro Rosso	1:40.074	1:39.296	1:39.277	5
6	20	Kevin Magnussen McLaren	1:39.735	1:39.022	1:39.629	11
7	3	Daniel Ricciardo Red Bull	1:40.519	1:39.666	1:39.635	6
8	14	Fernando Alonso Ferrari	1:40.255	1:39.786	1:39.709	7
9	7	Kimi Räikkönen Ferrari	1:40.098	1:39.838	1:39.771	8
10	25	Jean-Eric Vergne Toro Rosso	1:40.354	1:39.929	1:40.020	9

Kevin Magnussen, Nico Hülkenberg and Max Chilton - 5 place grid penalties for changing their gearboxes.

Pastor Maldonado - 5 place grid penalty carried over for exceeding his quota of five engine components at the Japanese Grand Prix. Plus a 5 place penalty after a gearbox change.

THE RACE

The race was overshadowed by concern for Jules Bianchi. There was an emotional tribute to the 25 year old Frenchman on the grid from both his team and the other drivers, with a minute's silence.

Lewis Hamilton made a great start, as did Rosberg, who was all over the back of his Mercedes team mate as they ran through the curve at Turn 1. As they both approached the tight right hander at Turn 2, Rosberg moved out of Hamilton's slipstream on the outside, but was travelling too fast and leaving his braking far too late. Lewis appeared to know that he had overcooked it and didn't challenge him, as Rosberg tried to return the favour that Hamilton has inflicted on him several times this season. Rosberg inevitably locked up really badly, smoke billowing from his front tyres. He gained the lead by cutting the corner and was informed by his team that he'd have to give the place back to Hamilton, but immediately informed them that by flat spotting his tyres he could hardly see with the vibrations caused by his hard braking and was going to have to pit at the end of the lap. Hamilton was quicker all weekend and most probably would have won, even if Rosberg could have overtaken him.

As per usual at all circuits, Pirelli had inspected the track earlier in the year in order to gauge what tyres they would bring to the race. However, the tarmac hadn't been laid at that point, so they couldn't test the tarmac for its grip levels. And so we were shown what a race would look like when tyre degradation hasn't been factored into Pirelli's choice of tyres, on a freshly laid and very smooth track that had superior grip levels - a procession. This was highlighted when Rosberg rejoined at the back of the pack, where he picked his way through the field and suddenly was in 3rd place, right behind Valtteri Bottas, after the leading cars made their one and only pit stops. Rosberg didn't have to stop again and did 52 laps on the same set of the harder medium tyres. At the front, Bottas was able to match the pace of Hamilton in the early stages of the race, but Hamilton gradually eked out a lead of 40 seconds before his pit stop on lap 27.

Rosberg meteoric rise through the field was indicative of the Mercedes' speed and on lap 31, Rosberg slipped inside Bottas in Turn 2 to move into 2nd, and despite Williams initial belief that Rosberg would have to stop again, he was able to hang on without much trouble, to the end. On lap 40 the team asked Rosberg if he could make it to the end on this set of tyres. Rosberg responds that it will be difficult, but he thinks it could be possible.

Despite being consistently fast, including setting the fastest lap of the race, and being on fresher tyres, he was unable to catch Hamilton. Towards the end, Rosberg was 20 seconds behind Hamilton, having put in a couple of quick laps to briefly close the gap a little, before Hamilton posted his own fastest lap to prove he was in control.

The McLarens had looked good all weekend and Button ran at a highest place of 3rd before finishing 4th ahead of his team mate Magnussen, who achieved his best finish since the season opener in March. McLaren moved ahead of Force India to 5th place in the Constructors' Championship. Alonso drove a consistent race to finish 6th after fending Ricciardo off in the latter stages. Ricciardo had earlier jumped ahead of Vettel during the pit stops and stayed ahead of him. Vettel was 8th. Räikkönen and Pérez rounded out the top 10. Kvyat, to the disappointment of his home fans went backwards from his promising qualifying position of 5th to get 14th.

Mercedes 9th 1-2 of the season meant they had won their first ever constructors' championship, but the Drivers' Championship is still wide open with only three races to go, and the double points in Abu Dhabi means it will probably go down to the wire. However, the threat of those double points altering the result artificially hangs heavily over Formula 1.

"It was a good day and an amazing weekend," Hamilton said after his win. "Firstly I'm so proud to have contributed to the work of this great team, to get the first Constructors' Championship for Mercedes-Benz is a huge achievement. Massive congratulations to the guys back in the UK and Germany, it's history for us. Today I had to manage the tyres a lot through the race, managing the fuel wasn't too bad. The car felt great and I didn't have to push too hard. At the end, when Nico was behind, I needed to match his times, which I did."

Rosberg was disappointed with his first lap error. "Today was a really tough race for me. I just messed up in the first corner. I simply braked too late, which was unnecessary. So I flat spotted my front tyres and it was impossible to continue due to the vibrations. I had to pit, and on the Prime tyre I had great pace. In the middle of the race I thought the degradation would start to increase. But very soon it was stable and I was able to push a lot. Then I managed to overtake Bottas. Also, still at the end I was able to push, but the team asked me to control the pace as everyone was worried about dropping at the very end of the race. P2 was damage limitation. I really look forward to the last 3 races of the year with this outstanding championship car."

"We went into the race today with the mentality that we were going to fight Mercedes for the win," said Bottas after his podium finish which moved him up to 4th in the championship, "but their pace in the race surprised us a bit and in the end we need to be satisfied with third place and another podium. I was keeping pace with Hamilton at the beginning but in the middle of my first stint the rear tyres started to go away and that allowed him to create a gap. In the second stint I didn't realize Rosberg was quite as close as he was and his move caught me a bit by surprise, but he had more pace at that point anyway as my prime tyres were taking a good ten laps to switch on so he would have caught me regardless. I was closing in the final laps as my tyres were getting better but he had managed to create too big a gap."

RUSSIAN GRAND PRIX 2014 RACE RESULT

Pos.	No.	Driver (Constructor)	Laps	Time	Grid	Points
1	44	**Lewis Hamilton Mercedes**	53	1:31:50.744	1	25
2	6	Nico Rosberg, Mercedes Mercedes	53	+13.657	2	18
3	77	Valtteri Bottas Williams-Mercedes	53	+17.425	3	15
4	22	Jenson Button McLaren-Mercedes	53	+30.234	4	12
5	20	Kevin Magnussen McLaren-Mercedes	53	+53.616	11	10
6	14	Fernando Alonso Ferrari	53	+1:00.016	7	8
7	3	Daniel Ricciardo Red Bull-Renault	53	+1:01.812	6	6
8	1	Sebastian Vettel Red Bull-Renault	53	+1:06.185	10	4
9	7	Kimi Räikkönen Ferrari	53	+1:18.877	8	2
10	11	Sergio Pérez Force India-Mercedes	53	+1:20.067	12	1

DRIVERS' CHAMPIONSHIP

Pos.	Driver	Points
1	Lewis Hamilton	291
2	Nico Rosberg	274
3	Daniel Ricciardo	199
4	Valtteri Bottas	145
5	Sebastian Vettel	143

CONSTRUCTORS' CHAMPIONSHIP

Pos.	Constructor	Points	
1	**Mercedes**	**565**	**2014 Constructors' Champions**
2	Red Bull-Renault	342	
3	Williams-Mercedes	216	
4	Ferrari	188	
5	McLaren-Mercedes	143	

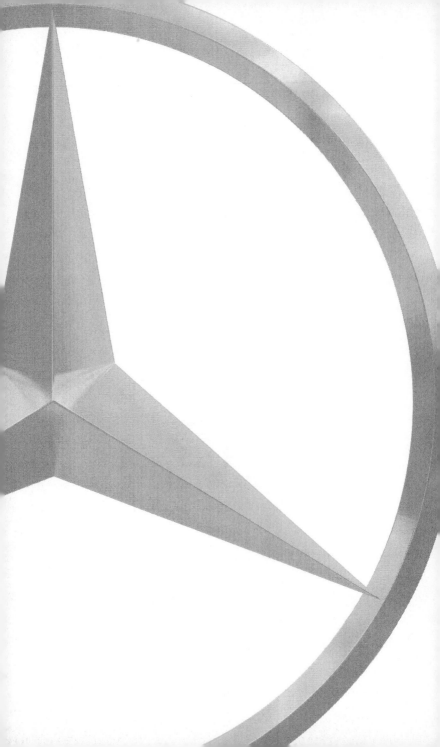

THE UNITED STATES GRAND PRIX

AUSTIN

ROUND 17
CIRCUIT OF THE AMERICAS
UNITED STATES GRAND PRIX

YEE-HAH!

HAMILTON MAKES IT A CAREER BEST OF 5 IN A ROW

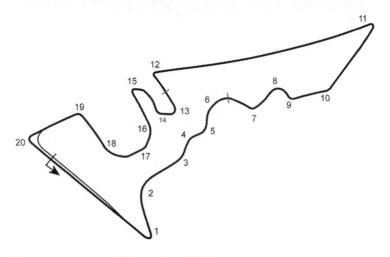

Date: 2 November 2014

Official Name: 2014 Formula 1 United States Grand Prix

Circuit: Circuit of the Americas, Travis County, Austin, Texas

Lap Length: 5.5 km (3.4 miles)

Lap Record: 1:39.347 - Sebastian Vettel (2012)

Distance: 56 laps, 308.4 km (191.6 miles)

THE RETURN OF THE SILVER ARROWS

The Marussia and Caterham teams are under administration and did not participate in the Grand Prix, and thus the race featured a field of only 18 cars, the smallest field that has gone into a Grand Prix since the 2005 Monaco Grand Prix. Because of this, instead of the six slowest cars being eliminated after the first and second rounds, only the slowest four were eliminated. Pirelli brought the white-walled Medium compound tyre as its prime selection and the yellow-walled soft tyre as the option, as opposed to the previous two meetings in Austin where the Hard and Medium compounds were selected. The FIA tested a new system in FP3, in response to minimising the risk of the kind of accident that Jules Bianchi suffered at the Japanese Grand Prix. Drivers have agreed it is a worthwhile system which needs a little tweaking.

QUALIFYING

Hamilton soon stamped his authority on Q1 with a 1m 38.795s lap, with Bottas, Rosberg and Massa, Sutil and Pérez trailing in his wake. 8 minutes in, Rosberg responded with a 1m 38.599s. Hulkenberg was 14th and on the bubble of missing the cut to Q2. Ricciardo was still in the pits while Vettel could only manage 10th. 3 minutes later, Rosberg lowered his time to 1m 38.303s. With 5 minutes left, Ricciardo was out and went 5th with a 1m 38.969s. Maldonado went into 4th place on the softer tyres. Alonso to second. Vettel got pushed down to 17th. Although with a new engine in his car, meaning he exceeded the 5 allotted for the season, he would have to start the race from the pits anyway. He had suggested that he wouldn't run at all until the race itself so as to save the engine, but pressure was put on him not to carry out the threat, and there was also the possibility that he could have been sanctioned by the Race officials if he had carried it out.

Hamilton then went fastest with a 1m 37.196s. The top 10 after Q1 were Hamilton, Massa, Bottas, Rosberg, Alonso, Magnussen, Button, Maldonado, Räikkönen and Ricciardo. The 4 drivers eliminated were Vergne, Gutierrez, Vettel and Grosjean.

In Q2 Kvyat set the first time of 1m 38.699s, beaten by Bottas, with 9 minutes left, with a 1m 38.094s, and then Rosberg went faster with a 1m 37.099s. Hamilton went 2nd with Alonso 3rd pushing Bottas down to 4th. 7 minutes to go and Hamilton reports he has a vibration from the tyres. The top 10 were now Rosberg, Hamilton, Alonso, Button, Magnussen, Bottas, Ricciardo, Räikkönen, Massa and Kvyat. With a minute to go,

Massa moved to 3rd with Bottas in 4th, as Kvyat fell to 12th. In the dying moments Rosberg did a 1m 36.290s to go top and the final top 10 was Rosberg, Hamilton, Massa, Bottas, Ricciardo, Alonso, Button, Magnussen, Räikkönen and Sutil. The 4 out were Maldonado, Pérez, Hulkenberg and Kvyat.

In Q3, Bottas set the time to beat with a 1m 36.906s. Hamilton beat that with a 1m 36.443s and then Rosberg bettered that with a 1m 36.282s. The order after the first runs was Rosberg, Hamilton, Bottas, Massa, Button, Magnussen, Alonso, Ricciardo, Räikkönen and Sutil. In the final moments, Rosberg set a 1m 36.067s to set provisional pole while Hamilton was 0.376 seconds slower. The top 10 for the grid was Rosberg, Hamilton, Bottas, Massa, Ricciardo, Alonso, Button, Magnussen, Räikkönen and Sutil. Hamilton now trails Rosberg 9-7 in the race for the Pole Position trophy in an area that Hamilton usually dominates and if Hamilton doesn't win pole in Brazil then Rosberg will win it.

QUALIFYING RESULT (Top 10)

Q3	Car No.	Driver (Constructor)	Q1 Time	Q2 Time	Q3 Time	Grid Pos.
1	**6**	**Nico Rosberg** **Mercedes**	**1:38.303**	**1:36.290**	**1:36.067**	**1**
2	44	Lewis Hamilton Mercedes	1:37.196	1:37.287	1:36.443	2
3	77	Valtteri Bottas Williams	1:38.249	1:37.499	1:36.906	3
4	19	Felipe Massa Williams	1:37.877	1:37.347	1:37.205	4
5	3	Daniel Ricciardo Red Bull	1:38.814	1:37.873	1:37.244	5
6	14	Fernando Alonso Ferrari	1:38.349	1:38.010	1:37.610	6
7	22	Jenson Button McLaren	1:38.574	1:38.024	1:37.655	12
8	20	Kevin Magnussen McLaren	1:38.557	1:38.047	1:37.706	7
9	7	Kimi Räikkönen Ferrari	1:38.669	1:38.263	1:37.804	8
10	99	Adrian Sutil Sauber-Ferrari	1:38.855	1:38.378	1:38.810	9

Jenson Button - 5 place grid penalty for a gearbox change.

Daniil Kvyat - 10 place grid penalty for an engine change.

Sebastian Vettel - starts from the pit lane after exceeding the season limit of 5 power unit component changes.

THE RACE

Rosberg led off the line as the lights went out and Hamilton settled into his wake. But on the opening lap Pérez rears Räikkönen, who then touches Adrian Sutil and Sutil is out. The safety car comes out and many of the drivers took the opportunity to pit. As the safety car comes in Rosberg continues to lead with Hamilton close behind.

As Rosberg is in the lead he has first refusal in making his pit stop first, which he did on lap 15. Hamilton came in one lap later and rejoined 2.8 seconds behind. Hamilton was on 'Hammer Time' and 5 laps later was within a second of Rosberg. On lap 24 he set the fastest first sector of the race so far, to put himself right up to Rosberg's rear wing as they turned into the tight right hander at Turn 11 before the main straight. Hamilton dived for the inside at Turn 12 and appeared to catch Rosberg daydreaming. He reacted in defence, but you cannot change direction in the braking zone, so he desists. Hamilton was on the inside and then they were side by side. Hamilton eased Rosberg wide onto the kerbs and gained the lead. Again Rosberg loses out to Hamilton in the close encounters - Rosberg has not won one of these battles all season and that may well be telling in the Championship race. Rosberg tried to stabilise the gap to Hamilton to around 1.4 seconds but eventually Hamilton extended it further. Rosberg briefly regained the lead on Hamilton's second stop, but again relinquished it during his own stop.

Ricciardo had dropped to 6th at the start but fought back strongly, passing Alonso after the safety car period. He then passed Bottas by making his first stop a lap earlier than the Finn, and did the same to Massa at the second stop, to come home 3rd behind the Mercedes, who were once again in a league of their own. It was another momentous drive by Ricciardo, who has emerged as a major star of the season, putting team mate and 4 time World Champion, Vettel to shame. "I'm happy with that," he said. "I could see the Mercedes for the first part of the race, which was really cool, I don't know if they were just chilling, but we seemed to have good pace. It was great to get ahead of the Williams and to get onto the podium. The start wasn't very good, I have to put my hand up to that one, but the recovery was good, so we didn't really lose out. The pit stops were really good, Red Bull is known for being awesome in the pits and they showed it today."

Massa came home in 4th, just ahead of his team mate, Bottas. Alonso was 6th, running a very long middle stint, and holding off a charging Vettel on the last lap. Vettel, having started the race from pit lane, looked to be the main beneficiary of the opening lap collision between Sutil and Pérez, pitting immediately for soft tyres from last place while the safety car held up the front runners. However, he ran over debris from the incident, and immediately had to switch back to the medium tyres. He made a late pit stop for a final set of softs and charged his way through the field, setting fastest lap when doing so, making 4 pit stops in all, but managed to finish in 7th place after passing Magnussen on the last lap, the only McLaren in the points, in 8th. Vergne made a hurried charge at the end of the race and made contact with Grosjean under heavy braking into Turn 1, but managed to finish in 9th place, only to receive a 5 second penalty for the avoidable contact on Grosjean, relegating him to 10th and allowing Pastor Maldonado into 9th, his first points for the season.

With his 10th win of the season to Rosberg's 4, Hamilton achieved 5 consecutive wins for the first time in his career and his 32nd win overall, breaking Nigel Mansell's record held since 1994, for the most wins for a British driver. With Ricciardo only finishing 3rd, it became mathematically impossible for him to win the Drivers' World Championship.

"What an incredible place this is to go racing," Hamilton said after his win. "We have such great support here and I have to say a massive thanks to the fans who have been awesome all weekend. I'm really grateful to have had the opportunity to be out front here. It's a very special feeling to have such an amazing car, an amazing team and to be on this incredible run. It's been an unbelievable job from the team all year, so a big thanks to everyone here at the track and at the factories back home. Coming here today, just having that same determination and hunger to get that win and, as I said, there's not a better crowd really to do that in front of. We managed to correct the problems from qualifying, which was great and I pushed as hard as I could. For the overtake, I just stayed as close as possible to Nico and waited for the moment to be just close enough to throw it up the inside. This is a good circuit to be able to follow another car but it's still not easy. You have to judge the risk in these situations but I felt confident I could pull it off. Once I got past Nico, it was just about controlling the race. I'm very, very proud to now hold the record for the most Formula 1 wins for a British driver. I have to say, though, it's all thanks to the team and the car we have this year that I've been able to reach that landmark so quickly. Ten wins in a season is just… well, wow!"

Hamilton has struck a huge psychological blow to Rosberg, who knew he needed 'three strong races' to have any chance of beating his team mate to the title. "It was a tough day for me and it feels horrible to finish second after starting from pole," he said. "The conditions were very different compared to yesterday and it took me too long to find my rhythm at the beginning. In Formula 1 it is all about adapting quickly, but it just took me too long. Only 10 laps after Lewis passed me, I got it right and was able to push much more. Lewis just did a better job today, so congratulations to him. It's getting tougher but there is still a chance for the title and everything can happen. I'm still going to be pushing flat out just as I always have. I never give up."

Hamilton also equalled the win tally of Fernando Alonso. They are now equal 5th on the all time Formula 1 winners' list. The 1978 world champion and 'sheriff for the day,' Mario Andretti was on the podium, in the role of the driver interviewer, and after initially refusing, eventually agreed to let the race winner borrow his Stetson!

UNITED STATES GRAND PRIX
2014 RACE RESULT

Pos.	No.	Driver (Constructor)	Laps	Time	Grid	Points
1	44	**Lewis Hamilton** **Mercedes**	56	1:40.785 2	25	
2	6	Nico Rosberg Mercedes	56	+4.314	1	18
3	3	Daniel Ricciardo Red Bull-Renault	56	+25.560	5	15
4	19	Felipe Massa Williams-Mercedes	56	+26.924	4	12
5	77	Valtteri Bottas Williams-Mercedes	56	+30.992	3	10
6	14	Fernando Alonso Ferrari	56	+1:35.231	6	8
7	1	Sebastian Vettel Red Bull-Renault	56	+1:35.734	PL	6
8	20	Kevin Magnussen McLaren-Mercedes	56	+1:40.682	7	4
9	13	Pastor Maldonado Lotus-Renault	56	+1:47.870	10	2
10	25	Jean-Éric Vergne Toro Rosso-Renault	56	+1:48.863	14	1

Jean-Éric Vergne - 5 seconds added to race time for making contact with Romain Grosjean while overtaking him.

DRIVERS' CHAMPIONSHIP

Pos.	Driver	Points
1	**Lewis Hamilton**	**316**
2	Nico Rosberg	292
3	Daniel Ricciardo	214
4	Valtteri Bottas	155
5	Sebastian Vettel	149

CONSTRUCTORS' CHAMPIONSHIP

Pos.	Constructor	Points
1	**Mercedes**	**608**
2	Red Bull-Renault	363
3	Williams-Mercedes	238
4	Ferrari	196
5	McLaren-Mercedes	147

THE BRAZILIAN GRAND PRIX

SÃO PAULO

ROUND 18
AUTODROMO JOSE CARLOS PACE
BRAZILIAN GRAND PRIX

ROSBERG KEEPS TITLE HUNT ALIVE
DOUBLE POINTS IN ABU DHABI GIVES HIM HOPE

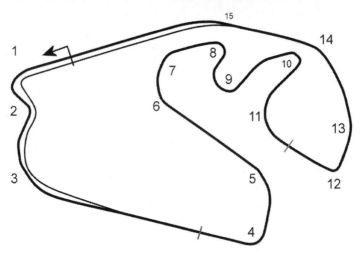

Date: 9 November 2014

Official Name: Formula 1 Grande Prêmio, Petrobras do Brasil

Circuit: Autódromo José Carlos Pace, São Paulo, Brazil

Lap Length: 4.3 km (2.7 miles)

Lap Record: 1:11.473 - Juan Pablo Montoya (2004)

Distance: 71 laps, 305.9 km (190.1 miles)

Marussia and Caterham again missed a Grand Prix after being granted dispensation from attending the event by Bernie Ecclestone, due to their financial woes, leaving the field again with 18 cars. The circuit had been resurfaced, with a much smoother tarmac. Following a series of accidents in national races, the pit lane was altered, with the entry brought forward from the Arquibancadas Corner to move it off the racing line and a chicane added to the pit lane to further slow cars entering the pits. The pit exit was moved further away from the circuit to allow for a run-off area on the outside of Turn 2. Pirelli originally nominated the orange-banded Hard and white-banded Medium tyres, as it has since 2012. However, following the Russian Grand Prix, many drivers criticised the high level of grip on the new tarmac of the Sochi Autodrom. With unanimous agreement with all 11 teams, Pirelli ultimately decided to bring the Medium and Soft tyres to the event.

QUALIFYING

Ricciardo topped the time sheets with a 1m 12.825s to set the benchmark in Q1. 6 minutes in and the Mercedes' boys were on their first run, Hamilton did a 1m 11.223s. Rosberg topped that with a 1m 10.693s. Hamilton responded 3 minutes later with a 1m 10.457s. Rosberg then replied with a 1m 10.347s. They were going for it hammer and tongs. Does that make Rosberg the tongs? Alonso was 3rd and Massa 4th. With 5 minutes left, Button went 3rd. A minute later, Ricciardo was struggling in 14th and Vettel hadn't come out yet. Massa was now 3rd in his home race with Bottas 4th, once again proving that in the 2nd half of the season they have been the best team behind Mercedes. The top 10 at the end of Q1 were Rosberg, Hamilton, Massa, Bottas, Button, Magnussen, Räikkönen, Kvyat, Gutierrez and Alonso. The 4 drivers eliminated were Grosjean, Vergne, Pérez and Maldonado.

Hamilton clocked a 1m 10.712s lap in Q2, and Rosberg soundly beat that with a 1m 10.303s. Massa was 3rd and Räikkönen 4th. With 4 minutes to go, the top 10 were Rosberg, Hamilton, Bottas, Massa, Button, Magnussen, Vettel, Räikkönen, Alonso and Hulkenberg. With 2 minutes left, most drivers began their final runs. The Mercedes' team mates, however, had done enough and stayed in the pits. As the session concluded, Massa went 2nd ahead of Bottas in 3rd. The top 10 in Q2 were Rosberg, Massa, Bottas, Hamilton, Button, Vettel, Räikkönen, Ricciardo, Magnussen and Alonso. The 4 drivers out were Gutierrez, Hulkenberg, Sutil and Kvyat.

Hamilton had now been outpaced by Rosberg all weekend and with 7 minutes left, Rosberg again beat his team mate as he turned in a 1m 10.166s to Hamilton's 1m 10.195s. With a minute to go, Bottas claimed 3rd with a 1m 10.305s immediately bettered by Massa with a 1m 10.247 to put him on the second row at his home Grand Prix, the place where he was so close to clinching the 2008 World Championship in a Ferrari. Button was 5th ahead of Magnussen, Vettel, Ricciardo, Räikkönen and Alonso. Now, with one minute to go everyone was winding up for their final runs with all 10 on track. Hamilton set a 1m 10.056s to claim provisional pole, but then Rosberg put in a 1m 10.023s to claim the pole and to give him a chance tomorrow to hone in on Hamilton's championship lead. Massa, to the crowd's sheer delight, was 3rd followed by Bottas, Button, Vettel, Magnussen, Alonso, Ricciardo and Räikkönen. Rosberg had now secured the Pole Position Trophy in its first year with his total against Hamilton at 10-7.

QUALIFYING RESULT (Top 10)

Q3	Car No.	Driver (Constructor)	Q1 Time	Q2 Time	Q3 Time	Grid Pos.
1	6	**Nico Rosberg** **Mercedes**	**1:10.347**	**1:10.303**	**1:10.023**	1
2	44	Lewis Hamilton Mercedes	1:10.457	1:10.712	1:10.056	2
3	19	Felipe MassA Williams	1:10.602	1:10.343	1:10.247	3
4	77	Valtteri Bottas Williams	1:10.832	1:10.421	1:10.305	4
5	22	Jenson Button McLaren	1:11.097	1:11.127	1:10.930	5
6	1	Sebastian Vettel Red Bull	1:11.880	1:11.129	1:10.938	6
7	20	Kevin Magnussen McLaren	1:11.134	1:11.211	1:10.969	7
8	14	Fernando Alonso Ferrari	1:11.558	1:11.215	1:10.977	8
9	3	Daniel Ricciardo Red Bull	1:11.593	1:11.208	1:11.075	9
10	7	Kimi Räikkönen Ferrari	1:11.193	1:11.188	1:11.099	10

Daniil Kvyat - 7 place grid penalty to complete 10 place penalty that carries over from the previous race.

Sergio Pérez - 7 place grid penalty for causing an avoidable accident.

THE RACE

The Drivers' Championship race is now solely about Hamilton and Rosberg with Ricciardo now mathematically unable to haul in Hamilton's lead, even though it's always been about the top two, since early on in the season. Rosberg came to Brazil knowing that the last two races of the season, realistically, would have to be his, if he was to have any chance of overhauling Hamilton's lead in the Championship. He'd given himself the best chance by securing his 10th pole position of the year but how often has he been caught and passed by Hamilton in the race, when it mattered? Could he resist him now?

Rosberg had been quickest all weekend including all 3 Free Practice sessions and grasped the lead at the start of the 71 lap race. He led for the first 6 laps and then pitted for the harder medium tyres. Hamilton led for two laps and then made his own first stop. Then Hulkenberg inherited the lead as he was on a different tyre strategy in his Force India, leading for 4 laps until he, too, pitted. Back in front on lap 14, Rosberg had 2 seconds over Hamilton. The lead swapped momentarily, Rosberg again pitted on lap 26 and Hamilton, who was now super fast and had been closing the gap on Rosberg , bringing it down to 1.1 seconds when Rosberg pitted for a second time. Hamilton now saw his opportunity, it was Hammer Time!! He posts the fastest lap of the race at 1m 14.303s but decides to stay out for another lap with his tyres now going off. He is still going faster but at Turn 4 he has a major spin and although he saves it, he loses over 7 seconds. He pits and comes out 7.4 seconds behind Rosberg. if he'd have come in after the first lap he probably would have come out of the pits wheel to wheel with Rosberg, if not slightly ahead.

Hamilton proved how quick he is by easily closing the gap and catching Rosberg. Rosberg led laps 29 to 49 and then made his 3rd and final stop. Hamilton led for 2 laps and then made his last stop. As Hamilton came out of the pits, Rosberg retook the lead on lap 52 and held on until the chequered flag to take the Championship race to the wire.

As for the sideshow, the fans cheered vociferously, as home hero Massa finished 3rd in his Williams to continue his fine end to the season. He had an eventful race, which included a pit lane speeding penalty, pitting in the McLaren pit by mistake, and some gripping wheel to wheel action on the track. "It was not an easy race but what a fantastic result for me, for my family, and for the team to finish on the podium in front of my home fans," he said. "The energy from the crowd was amazing and really pushed me forward. The car had strong and consistent pace today and this allowed me to stay in third despite issues in my two pit stops. In the first stop I incurred a stop-and-go penalty after speeding in the pit lane after I hit the limiter twice by mistake, and in the second, I stopped in the wrong box. We're not normally next to McLaren and in their light overalls, looked the same colour as ours, so this caught me out. In the end these issues were not enough to take away my podium because we had a good aggressive strategy and a really good car." The two incidents lost him some time, but he was able to hold off McLaren's Jenson Button. As McLaren deliberate over whether to choose Button or Magnussen to partner Alonso next season, the 2009 World Champion has again proved that he can drag an uncompetitive car into a decent position and has outscored his team mate, Magnussen all season, who was a disappointing 9th. Button was initially behind Bottas in 4th place, but the unfortunate Finn suffered two slow pit stops, including one where he had to have his seatbelts tightened. "It was a race full of different problems for me and in the end it just wasn't my day," Bottas said. "I had an issue with my belts at the beginning that we resolved at the first pit stop but this lost me a lot of time and I also lost time in the second stop. The conditions were very challenging as tyre wear was high and all cars were experiencing graining."

"It all went pretty smoothly until my final pit stop," said Button, "there was a bit of miscommunication about stopping, which meant I ended up doing an extra lap. That could have cost us a chance of the podium. It's a shame we couldn't hang on to Felipe, but it was still a fantastic race."

Sebastian Vettel was 5th in his Red Bull. "I had a good launch at the start, and then into Turn 4... maybe I don't have the best memories of Turn 4 here from two years ago, I didn't know how aggressive Kevin was going to be going into it and I left a bit too much space. I went a bit wide and lost two positions as I couldn't get on the power out of the corner. Then I had to fight hard to get the positions back during the race which we did, especially with the strategy. I hoped to get maybe one more position to finish fourth, but in the end it was a good result for us here." Just behind was McLaren bound Alonso, "After a far from easy weekend, I am reasonably pleased with the outcome of the race, because even if we weren't very competitive, we managed to score a good number of points. Today, degradation was particularly high, especially in the first stint on the softs, which lasted less time than expected because of graining. When I passed Kimi, my tyres were newer than his, as he was on a two stop, but I was having to save fuel and after that overtaking move, there was nothing more I could do. Now there's just one race to go this season and in terms of the Constructors' Championship, we hope to manage to keep McLaren behind us in the final race in Abu Dhabi. As for myself, I reckon I'm in the position I deserve, because others have done better."

Hulkenberg was a credible 8th. "It was quite a cool race and very satisfying to finish in eighth," Hulkenberg said. "With a three-stop race you are always pushing, but my race was not too complicated and I was on my own for a large part of the afternoon. I also had a few nice battles and it was good fun. The car felt a bit better today compared to earlier in the weekend so I was more comfortable and really able to push." Meanwhile, Ricciardo, retired on lap 39 with a suspension failure.

Hamilton now holds a 17 point lead over Rosberg in the Championship. The permutations are numerable but with double points available in the last race and with the Mercedes' record this season, Hamilton has to come 2nd if Rosberg wins or obviously just beat Rosberg in Abu Dhabi to win the Drivers' Championship. "That was a fantastic weekend and I felt very comfortable over the whole three days," Rosberg said after his 5th win of the season. "I had to learn from Austin, which was a big disappointment, and I think I achieved that. I was able to control the pace a bit better and didn't let Lewis come too close. He drove really well and was always right there pushing me."

Hamilton was clearly disappointed by his spin. "I think ultimately it cost me the win," Hamilton admitted. "I was much quicker up until that point and on that lap I'd gone a second quicker whilst Nico pitted and I thought I was going to pit at the end of that lap so I used everything of the tyres. The next lap, I had nothing left. Either way, at the end of the day, I made a mistake. I locked the rears into Turn 4 and with the under rotation, just spun me around. Second time it's happened this weekend. So, no-one's fault but mine."

"It was important for me to just improve," Rosberg added, "because I just didn't do a good enough job in the race in Austin. Today I managed to do that, so that, I'm happy about. I learned from Austin and did better so that's a big step in the right direction. One race too late but there's still all to play for. Now I'm just hoping for, and need to try and keep this going now. Really feeling good in the car and everything. And it was a great race with Lewis. He had a great race too, just behind me all the time. I always needed to make sure that the gap was always such that there was no chance for him to go for the overtake - unlike Austin. And I managed to do that, so that was good."

BRAZILIAN GRAND PRIX 2014 RACE RESULT

Pos.	No.	Driver (Constructor)	Laps	Time	Grid	Points
1	6	**Nico Rosberg** Mercedes	71	**1:30:02.555**	1	25
2	44	Lewis Hamilton Mercedes	71	+1.457	2	18
3	19	Felipe Massa Williams-Mercedes	71	+41.031	3	15
4	22	Jenson Button McLaren-Mercedes	71	+48.658	5	12
5	1	Sebastian Vettel Red Bull-Renault	71	+51.420	6	10
6	14	Fernando Alonso Ferrari	71	+1:01.906	8	8
7	7	Kimi Räikkönen Ferrari	71	+1:03.730	10	6
8	27	Nico Hülkenberg Force India-Mercedes	71	+1:03.934	12	4
9	20	Kevin Magnussen McLaren-Mercedes	71	+1:10.085	7	2
10	77	Valtteri Bottas Williams-Mercedes	70	+1 Lap	4	1

DRIVERS' CHAMPIONSHIP

Pos. Driver   Points

1 **Lewis Hamilton** **334**
2 **Nico Rosberg**   **317**   2014 Pole Position Trophy
3 Daniel Ricciardo   214
4 Sebastian Vettel   159
5 Fernando Alonso   157

CONSTRUCTORS' CHAMPIONSHIP

Pos.	Constructor	Points
1	**Mercedes**	**651**
2	Red Bull-Renault	373
3	Williams-Mercedes	254
4	Ferrari	210
5	McLaren-Mercedes	161

THE ABU DHABI GRAND PRIX

YAS MARINA

ROUND 19
YAS MARINA CIRCUIT
ABU DHABI GRAND PRIX

OK LEWIS, IT'S HAMMER TIME!!

HAMILTON CROWNED CHAMPION AS GRACIOUS ROSBERG FINISHES 14TH

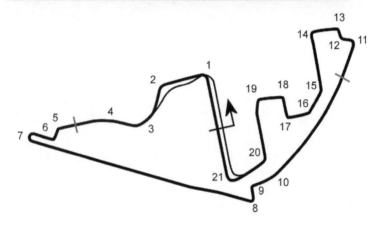

Date: 23 November 2014

Official Name: 2014 Formula 1 Etihad Airways, Abu Dhabi Grand Prix

Circuit: Yas Marina Circuit, Yas Island, Abu Dhabi, United Arab Emirates

Lap Length: 5.5 km (3.4 miles)

Lap Record: 1:40.279 - Sebastian Vettel (2009)

Distance: 55 laps, 305.4 km (189.7 miles)

Abu Dhabi is the only day-night race that has appeared on the Formula 1 calendar, ever. It starts at 5pm in the day and continues through sunset, when the drivers have the added distraction of the sun going down over the circuit, often shining directly into their eyes. It ends in darkness as the sun sets very quickly. For the first time in Formula 1, teams and drivers will score double points for the last race. This was in order to prolong any championship battle till the final race. Even if you look at the 4 years of Vettel's championship domination, only 2 were decided before the denouement. Bernie Ecclestone originally wanted double points for the all of the last 3 races of the season, but the teams agreed one was enough. The rule change has been roundly criticised by the teams, the drivers and the fans, as potentially it could artificially manipulate who is the champion. Lewis Hamilton has clearly been the best driver of the year, not only with his superior race pace but for his wheel to wheel race craft, where he has completely dominated Rosberg, and has often negated Rosberg's superior qualifying record, the only place where Nico has beaten Lewis. If the order is Rosberg first and Hamilton third, for instance, then Rosberg will be champion on double points. In the old system Hamilton would still be 7 points ahead! This would leave Formula 1 under a cloud in a season that there have been many storms. "I don't have a fear but I think the last race with the double points has the potential to overshadow a season," said Mercedes boss Toto Wolff. "We know why the double points came and it made all the sense in the world, to make it spectacular for the audience, the fans and the viewers, but now we are in a situation that it could change the outcome."

Hamilton will approach the race exactly as he has approached all the races this year, with 120% effort, and is fairly sanguine. "It doesn't really change, same as for Nico really, because we're hunting for those points." Rosberg is happier with the offer of 50 points in the race, "It's great to hear of course, because then there's a definite shot at the championship this year, even with the points that I'm now behind."

Marussia did not contest the Grand Prix as a bid to save the team from completely going under failed, forcing the team to close down. They had made a last minute attempt to race in Abu Dhabi, with suggestions that a potential investor was interested in the team. However, the deal fell through, ending their chances of making a return to the grid. In the same situation, Caterham successfully attempted to raise funds through fans to attend the race, which ultimately proved successful and the team returned for the final act, bringing the grid up to 20 cars. Ericsson had terminated his contract with Caterham a week and a half before the race, so while they retained Kobayashi for the race, Caterham hired the young 23 year old British driver, Will Stevens (who was their test driver for the latter part of last season), as their 2nd driver. Pirelli will supply the Yellow-banded Soft tyre as the Prime, while the Red-banded Supersoft will be the Option. The previous 3 seasons saw the Medium and Soft selections used.

QUALIFYING

With only 20 cars competing for qualifying, only 5 drivers will be eliminated at the end of Q1. So it's the final qualifying session of the season, which for championship rivals Lewis Hamilton and Nico Rosberg has been a topsy-turvy one, and the tension is palpable. Rosberg needs to win in the battle for the only thing he has dominated this season, he has to get pole to sow the seeds of doubt in his team mate.

Magnussen set the marker with a time of 1m 43.171s. Bottas goes faster with a 1m 42.436s. With 15 minutes to go, Rosberg goes for it, he has nothing to lose, and so much to gain, and turns in a decent 1m 41.308s. But Hamilton beats him with a 1m 41.207s using the super soft tyres. 10 minutes in, Vettel and Ricciardo head out, historically fast on this circuit. Bottas is 3rd, followed by Kvyat and Massa. With 4 minutes left, Vettel goes 4th, with Ricciardo 3rd. Alonso is 11th and Räikkönen 5th. Button is up to 3rd. Top 10 after Q1 are Hamilton, Rosberg, Massa, Magnussen, Button, Ricciardo, Kvyat, Bottas, Vergne and Räikkönen. The 5 drivers out are Grosjean, Gutierrez, Maldonado, Kobayashi and Stevens.

Massa is first to post a benchmark time of 1m 41.575s. Hamilton goes top 4 minutes in with a 1m 40.920s while Rosberg spins and is only 12th. Next time round he gets it right and goes 2nd with a 1m 41.459s. 6 minutes to go, Button and Magnussen had yet to set times, Button had been out but was called back because he didn't have enough fuel. "Are you serious?" he retorted over the radio in his best McEnroe-esque style. 2 minutes left and Button, Sutil, Magnussen and most of the rest are out. Magnussen is now 9th with Button 6th after refuelling. Räikkönen is 10th. So, the top 10 are Hamilton, Massa, Bottas, Rosberg, Ricciardo, Button, Alonso, Kvyat, Vettel and Räikkönen. The 5 out are Magnussen, Vergne, Pérez, Hulkenberg and Sutil.

So, here we are, after 18 qualifying sessions and at the last qualifying session of the 19th, the first part of the last part of the championship is

THE RETURN OF THE SILVER ARROWS

about to begin, and someone is going to have a psychological edge tomorrow. Hamilton has topped Q1 and Q2 and must feel confident that he can take one step closer to his 2nd World Championship. This is the best time for Nico to attack in order to burst Lewis' bubble and to ask some questions.

Vettel set the pace at 1m 42.164s which Bottas beat with 1m 41.321s, which Rosberg beat with a 1m 40.697s. Hamilton's turn, and he slides off but saves it and is 2nd with a 1m 41.021s. The order after the first runs is Rosberg, Hamilton, Massa, Bottas, Ricciardo, Vettel, Button, Alonso, Kvyat and Räikkönen. With 4 minutes to go and Vettel and Ricciardo are out for their final runs. Rosberg leaves his garage before Hamilton. Bottas gets 3rd with a 1m 41.025s while Rosberg improves on his time to hold on to provisional pole with a 1m 40.480s. Hamilton crosses the line and has improved his time but is short by nearly 4 tenths with a 1m 40.866s and it's all over. Rosberg's 11th pole position of the season. Hamilton has to settle for 2nd, with Bottas 3rd. Massa, Ricciardo, Vettel, Kvyat, Button, Räikkönen and Alonso round out the top 10. The first blow goes to Nico and now he has to do what he did in Brazil, convert a pole position into a race win - if he had done that all season, he would be leading the Championship. But you just cannot underestimate Lewis' determination and tenacity. He just won't give in! He's a fighter and he's proved it this year - proved that he can come back stronger after serious setbacks, particularly at Silverstone in the British Grand Prix when he was so down after qualifying.

Vettel and Ricciardo were excluded from qualifying after their cars were found to have front wings that flexed under an aerodynamic load more than allowed by the sporting regulations, 6 hours after the qualifying session. They were relegated to the back of the grid. They had to now change the front wings, which is a Parc Fermé violation and so were penalised again, having to start from the pit lane.

213

QUALIFYING RESULT (Top 10)

Q3	Car No.	Driver (Constructor)	Q1 Time	Q2 Time	Q3 Time	Grid Pos.
1	**6**	**Nico Rosberg Mercedes**	**1:41.308**	**1:41.459**	**1:40.480**	**1**
2	44	Lewis Hamilton Mercedes	1:41.207	1:40.920	1:40.866	2
3	77	Valtteri Bottas Williams	1:42.346	1:41.376	1:41.025	3
4	19	Felipe Massa Williams	1:41.475	1:41.144	1:41.119	4
5	26	Daniil Kvyat Toro Rosso	1:42.302	1:42.082	1:41.908	5
6	22	Jenson Button McLaren	1:42.137	1:41.875	1:41.964	6
7	7	Kimi Räikkönen Ferrari	1:42.439	1:42.168	1:42.236	7
8	14	Fernando Alonso Ferrari	1:42.467	1:41.940	1:42.866	8
11	20	Kevin Magnussen McLaren	1:42.104	1:42.198	NTS*	9
12	25	Jean-Eric Vergne Toro Rosso	1:42.413	1:42.207	NTS*	10

Romain Grosjean - demoted 4 grid places as part of 20 place penalty for using his 6th power unit of the season.

Daniel Ricciardo and Sebastian Vettel - excluded from the qualifying results and were relegated to the back of the grid for illegal front wings, and for violation of Parc Fermé conditions have to start from the pit lane.

* NTS (No Time Set in Q3) As a consequence of Red Bull's disqualification, Kevin Magnussen and Jean-Éric Vergne took 9th and 10th on the grid although they didn't take part in Q3.

THE RACE

You can cut the tension with a knife at the Yas Marina Circuit. Is there another twist in the tale? The straight forward equation barring mechanical failures is that Rosberg, needs to win and hope Hamilton finishes lower than second in order to win the title.

At the start Hamilton absolutely nails it and rockets off the grid. With Rosberg seeming to bog down, Hamilton is considerably ahead before the braking zone at the first corner with Rosberg almost losing a place to Massa. Bottas, too, had a bad start after qualifying in 3rd and dropped to 8th due to a slipping clutch. So a perfect start for Lewis and a disaster for Nico. Hamilton was some 1.2 seconds in front as they rounded the Yas Marina circuit for the first time, and gradually increased that lead until he was 2.7 seconds in front by the time he made his first pit stop on lap 10. Hamilton is now in complete control, and barring any mishaps is charging to his 2nd World Championship. The gap stayed consistent until around half-way on lap 23 when disaster struck for Rosberg. Rosberg was now putting in some pretty slow laps and reported on the radio that he was losing power as his Mercedes suffered a failure of the energy recovery system. From then on, it was a matter of damage limitation for Rosberg. He was lacking 160bhp for 33 seconds of the lap. Rosberg was simply impotent as he slipped down the field, exacerbated by brake problems associated to his power problems. When down to 7th on lap 34 he was still thinking of the Championship. "How's it looking, to be in the position I need if Lewis has a problem?" Rosberg asked his engineer. "It's not looking good, Nico," his engineer Tony Ross replied. "What the hell does that mean?" Rosberg frustratingly replied. "What times do I need to do?" "Just drive flat out," he was told.

Rookie Brit, Will Stevens, in the Caterham, had an exciting debut battling Alonso along the back straight when the Ferrari struggled with the Caterham's straight line speed before Alonso finally overtook him at Turn 8.

After Rosberg lost power, Mercedes put Hamilton's car into conservative settings but Hamilton was now thinking of the Championship and was aware that his car, too, could hit trouble. "Please don't turn up the car - I am comfortable. I can go faster if I need to."

With Massa in a comfortable 2nd, Williams decided that they would go for it to try and cap a superb season off with a win. At the 2nd set of pit stops

Williams put the supersofts on Massa's car for the final stint to try and reel in the 13 second lead that Hamilton now had with 12 laps to go. Massa closed that gap to 9 seconds with 8 laps to go and was taking around a second a lap out of Hamilton. But Hamilton was in complete control knowing that he could now go out of the race and still win the Championship with Rosberg down in 14th. But that isn't Lewis Hamilton's way, he wants to win the race to go out on a high and win the Championship in style. He controlled his pace and towards the end the gap stabilised around 2 to 3 seconds as Massa tyres began to go off. Williams took a fantastic double podium with Bottas in third after he recovered from his bad start, ahead of Ricciardo, who again drove a superb race to take 4th after starting from the pit lane, to complete an amazing first year at Red Bull. Button took 5th for McLaren in what could turn out to be the final curtain on his Formula 1 career. The Force Indias again had a strong showing on a different tyre strategy to take a 6th and 7th with Hulkenberg and Pérez respectively.

With 2 laps left, Rosberg was told to retire, but admirably replied, "I would like to go to the end." As Hamilton crossed the line, Prince Harry, who was a guest of Red Bull for the weekend, took to the team radio to say "Lewis, well done for not making the British public sweat. You are an absolute legend." Hamilton stood on his car to wildly celebrate and embraced his girlfriend Nicole Scherzinger (who kissed him on the helmet) and his family, who had chosen not to attend the race, but had changed their minds and flown in that morning to support him. It was Hamilton's 11th win of the season, to Rosberg's 5, eventually finishing 67 points clear of his rival, and is a deserved champion after driving aggressively all season long.

Rosberg was gracious in defeat and now that the battle was over the bad blood between the two appears to have subsided. "All in all, Lewis deserved to win the championship," Rosberg said. "What happened to me had no impact in the final result, it did not change anything, so there is no point focusing on that. He did just a little bit better than me. The positive is I've been the better qualifier over the last two years and that gives me a good base. I came very close and it is a pity it did not work out. I'm proud to have been here with the team. It's been very intense, a very special weekend for me, with so much support."

"Nico put on an incredible fight throughout the year," Hamilton said. "He was a phenomenal competitor. We met each other back in 1997 and we always said it would be amazing to be racing in the same team. He did an amazing job today and very sad obviously to know that his car wasn't quick enough, so that we can fight at the end. But still he was graceful enough to come up to me just now." Rosberg was granted permission to go to the private room where they hold the top 3 drivers before they go onto the podium. "He just came into the room - very, very professional, and I just said fantastic." Hamilton added. "He said 'you drove really well'. And the same to him, all year long he drove incredibly well, especially in qualifying, so hats off to him."

"I was asking the team if I could turn down the power," Hamilton said. "When the gap started to increase between me and Nico, I was thinking OK, I've got to back off, got to look after the tyres. So look after the car, started avoiding curbs, all those kind of things. A couple of moments down the straight I was rubbing the cockpit, I was saying 'come on baby, we can make it. Stick with me'. I really did. You won't see it but I did. Several times. But the car was feeling good and ultimately at the end I was able to push, I wanted to win the race, I wanted to have that battle with Felipe Massa. He obviously came in for those tyres and I thought, 'He's going to catch and get the win,' but managed to just keep him behind me."

Massa was clearly delighted that he had pushed the Mercedes to the end. "It was a close race," he said. "I didn't think the victory was there, but it was so close at the end. It was good to be racing and pushing the Mercedes. I hope this is a strong building block to go on for next year. The team progressed so much throughout the year, which is why we were able to get podiums in the second half of the season. We will continue this forward movement into next year." His team mate, Bottas, rounded off the top 3. "We were very competitive today," he said. "I got a bad start and the race was compromised after I was stuck behind a few cars, so to walk away with a podium is incredible. It was a good race, I could really push and fight. The team has grown and developed throughout the season, from our first race in Melbourne to our best result here. It's a great start to build on for next year and to continue the team's great history."

Hamilton is Britain's first multiple world champion in 43 years. Jackie Stewart last achieved the feat in 1971 and would win the title for a third and final time in 1973. Hamilton's six-year wait between titles (2008 to 2014) just falls short of Niki Lauda's record of seven (1977 to 1984) although he retired from the sport in 1979, returning in 1982. Graham Hill (1962, 1968) and Jack Brabham (1960, 1966) also had six-year gaps between title wins. Jackie Stewart (1969, 1971, 1973), Graham Hill (1962, 1968) and Jim Clark (1963, 1965) are Britain's only other multiple

F1 world champions. Hamilton becomes Mercedes' first champion since Juan Manuel Fangio's back-to-back titles for the manufacturer in 1954 and 1955.

Ricciardo had had great fun in storming to 4th from the pit lane. "I think it was pretty much a faultless race from all sides," he said, "from the strategy, to me and the pit stops, everything was good so we did everything we needed to. I had fun passing, it wasn't boring out there, so it was pretty much what I asked for. One spot better would have been nice, but fourth is really cool from the pit lane. It's been pretty much a perfect season, as perfect as it can be without holding a world title, so no real regrets, no complaints. It's nice to not only start the season well, but to finish it well also and I think all the way through it was good - we had a strong summer as well, so the start, middle and end were pretty good!"

In his last race in the Red Bull colours before moving to Ferrari Red, Vettel managed only 8th. "I felt there was more," he said, "but once I got stuck behind Kevin at the beginning it was quite tough, so I can't be completely happy with today. When you race, you want to finish as high up as you can and today I think we had the pace to finish higher. The last six years have been an incredible journey, obviously we didn't expect that when we started working together - you can never expect four driver titles and four constructors' championships in a row. You get to know some people in a very good way and build friendships that will last a long time. You go through happy days and sad days, you go through them together and I think I learned a lot."

Button once again made McLaren scratch their heads over the decision they have to make regarding Button's future when he brought the uncompetitive McLaren home in 5th. "That was tough!" he said. "I think we made the best of what we had this evening. In terms of strategy, we did the right thing, but we never really had enough pace to attack the cars in front. So, fifth was as good as it was going to be. Getting the maximum from the car is all that can be asked of a racing driver, and I think I've proved this year that I'm still at the top of my game. Since it's the last race of the season, I'd like to say a huge 'thanks' to Tom and Bernie, my two race engineers, who've done a fantastic job this year, as have all my mechanics. The whole team has been so supportive, which is lovely. It's been a good day for me, but a much better day for my old team buddy Lewis. Winning two world titles is an absolutely amazing achievement. Congratulations to him - he deserves it. I'm sure tonight will be fun - I'll celebrate a good end to the year with my family."

Force India's Nico Hülkenberg and Sergio Pérez came home a fighting 6th and 7th. "After struggling with the car on Friday and in qualifying, I think we can be proud of today's race and our performance is a good sign for next year as well," Hulkenberg said. "The car performed at its best. I had a good balance and I had the confidence to really push. There were just a few laps after the pit stops when I was managing the tyres, but other than that it was flat out all the way. The long final stint on the super soft tyres was brave, but it turned out to be a great strategy by the team and it really worked out well." Pérez said, "If we had been on the super soft tyres a bit earlier then maybe we could have been closer to Button at the end of the race. Looking back at the season overall I think everyone in the team has done a tremendous job and we should feel very happy about what we have achieved. I've enjoyed this season and now that I know the team I'm looking forward to coming back stronger in 2015."

Ferrari, however were not so happy with 9th and 10th. "Today," Alonso said, "my time with Ferrari comes to an end, as does a very tricky season, in which, even if we were unable to do much against the technical dominance of our rivals, we fought all the way to the very end, all of us did our utmost, putting our hearts into it. Today's race was difficult to manage but at the same time it was very emotional for me. After five years it's not easy to say farewell to a team with which I have grown so much over the past five years, both as a driver and as a person. I thank all the Ferraristi for their support. I will miss the team, the fans and Italy. Even though we are going our separate ways, I feel I have lived through a unique experience which any Formula 1 driver would have loved to have had." Räikkönen, on his race, said, "It was a very difficult race but we knew right from the beginning that this track would be tough for us. The start was good but then, at the first stop, I already lost a few places and from then on I couldn't move up the order. The car handled well and I had no particular problem, but today we lacked the speed we needed to attack. All season we have faced a series of difficulties which we put a lot of effort into solving and we learned a lot from that. We know which direction we need to work in to be competitive as soon as possible and I have absolute faith in the team."

But there was a happy man on the podium, a man with the grin of a Cheshire cat and he certainly had just got the cream. "It's very hard to soak all this up," said the 2014 World Champion. "When you're going through the race, when you're coming here this weekend, there's so much pressure from around you, you're just trying to ignore it, trying to keep your eye on the ball. I just cannot believe how amazing this has all been. Coming to this team last year, the decision to come here, when a lot of people said it was the wrong choice. The steps we took last year and then coming into this year, it was just unbelievable and then again, as I said, the fan support has been phenomenal. I never in a million years thought I'd have that kind of support, so, as I said before, this is the greatest moment in my life. It's very hard to... it feels very surreal. It feels like an out-of-body experience. I feel like I'm back here watching this going on, it's not really happening. So I'm going to really make sure I give my thanks and count my blessings."

Lewis said that he has asked to keep car number 44 for next year, even though he is entitled to the Number 1. Number 44 is the number he raced under in his Karting days. But today he is Number 1!

ABU DHABI GRAND PRIX 2014 RACE RESULT

Pos.	No.	Driver (Constructor)	Laps	Time	Grid	Points
1	44	**Lewis Hamilton Mercedes**	55	1:39:02.619	2	50
2	19	Felipe Massa Williams-Mercedes	55	+2.576	4	36
3	77	Valtteri Bottas Williams-Mercedes	55	+28.880	3	30
4	3	Daniel Ricciardo Red Bull-Renault	55	+37.237	PL	24
5	22	Jenson Button McLaren-Mercedes	55	+1:00.334	6	20
6	27	Nico Hülkenberg Force India-Mercedes	55	+1:02.148	12	16
7	11	Sergio Pérez Force India-Mercedes	55	+1:11.060	11	12
8	1	Sebastian Vettel Red Bull-Renault	55	+1:12.045	PL	8
9	14	Fernando Alonso Ferrari	55	+1:25.813	8	4
10	7	Kimi Räikkönen Ferrari	55	+1:27.820	7	2

DRIVERS' CHAMPIONSHIP 2014
(FINAL STANDINGS)

	Driver	Car No.	Points
1	**Lewis Hamilton** **2014 World Drivers' Champion**	**44**	**384**
2	Nico Rosberg	6	317
3	Daniel Ricciardo	3	238
4	Valtteri Bottas	77	186
5	Sebastian Vettel	1	167
6	Fernando Alonso	14	161
7	Felipe Massa	19	134
8	Jenson Button	22	126
9	Nico Hülkenberg	27	96
10	Sergio Pérez	11	59
11	Kevin Magnussen	20	55
12	Kimi Räikkönen	7	55
13	Jean-Éric Vergne	25	22
14	Romain Grosjean	8	8
15	Daniil Kvyat	26	8
16	Pastor Maldonado	13	2
17	Jules Bianchi	17	2
18	Adrian Sutil	99	0
19	Marcus Ericsson	9	0
20	Esteban Gutiérrez	21	0
21	Max Chilton	4	0
22	Kamui Kobayashi	10	0
23	Will Stevens	46	0

2014 DRIVER'S CHAMPIONSHIP TABLE

Pos.	Driver	No.	AUS	MAL	BHR	CHN	ESP	MON	CAN
1	UK **Lewis Hamilton**	44	Ret	1	1	1	1	2	Ret
2	GER **Nico Rosberg**	6	1	2	2	2	2	1	2
3	AUS **Daniel Ricciardo**	3	DSQ	Ret	4	4	3	3	1
4	FIN **Valtteri Bottas**	77	5	8	8	7	5	Ret	7
5	GER **Sebastian Vettel**	1	Ret	3	6	5	4	Ret	3
6	SPA **Fernando Alonso**	14	4	4	9	3	6	4	6
7	BRA **Felipe Massa**	19	Ret	7	7	15	13	7	12#
8	UK **Jenson Button**	22	3	6	17#	11	11	6	4
9	GER **Nico Hülkenberg**	27	6	5	5	6	10	5	5
10	MEX **Sergio Pérez**	11	10	DNS	3	9	9	Ret	11#
11	DEN **Kevin Magnussen**	20	2	9	Ret	13	12	10	9
12	FIN **Kimi Räikkönen**	7	7	12	10	8	7	12	10
13	FRA **Jean-Éric Vergne**	25	8	Ret	Ret	12	Ret	Ret	8
14	FRA **Romain Grosjean**	8	Ret	11	12	Ret	8	8	Ret
15	RUS **Daniil Kvyat**	26	9	10	11	10	14	Ret	Ret
16	VEN **Pastor Maldonado**	13	Ret	Ret	14	14	15	DNS	Ret
17	FRA **Jules Bianchi**	17	NC	Ret	16	17	18	9	Ret
18	GER **Adrian Sutil**	99	11	Ret	Ret	Ret	17	Ret	13
19	SWE **Marcus Ericsson**	9	Ret	14	Ret	20	20	11	Ret
20	MEX **Esteban Gutiérrez**	21	12	Ret	Ret	16	16	Ret	14#
21	UK **Max Chilton**	4	13	15	13	19	19	14	Ret
22	JAP **Kamui Kobayashi**	10	Ret	13	15	18	Ret	13	Ret
23	UK **Will Stevens**	46							
	GER **André Lotterer**	45							

\# Drivers did not finish the Grand Prix, but completed more than 90% of the race distance and were therfore classified in the race results.

RACE RESULTS AT A GLANCE

					Grand Prix							Points
AUT	GBR	GER	HUN	BEL	ITA	SIN	JPN	RUS	USA	BRA	ABU*	
2	1	3	3	Ret	1	1	1	1	1	2	1	384
1	Ret	1	4	2	2	Ret	2	2	2	1	14	317
8	3	6	1	1	5	3	4	7	3	Ret	4	238
3	2	2	8	3	4	11	6	3	5	10	3	186
Ret	5	4	7	5	6	2	3	8	7	5	8	167
5	6	5	2	7	Ret	4	Ret	6	6	6	9	161
4	Ret	Ret	5	13	3	5	7	11	4	3	2	134
11	4	8	10	6	8	Ret	5	4	12	4	5	126
9	8	7	Ret	10	12	9	8	12	Ret	8	6	96
6	11	10	Ret	8	7	7	10	10	Ret	15	7	59
7	7	9	12	12	10	10	14	5	8	9	11	55
10	Ret	11	6	4	9	8	12	9	13	7	10	55
Ret	10	13	9	11	13	6	9	13	10	13	12	22
14	12	Ret	Ret	Ret	16	13	15	17	11	17#	13	8
Ret	9	Ret	14	9	11	14	11	14	15	11	Ret	8
12	17#	12	13	Ret	14	12	16	18	9	12	Ret	2
15	14	15	15	18†	18	16	20#					2
13	13	Ret	11	14	15	Ret	21#	16	Ret	16	16	0
18	Ret	18	Ret	17	19	15	17	19				0
19	Ret	14	Ret	15	20	Ret	13	15	14	14	15	0
17	16	17	16	16	Ret	17	18	Ret				0
16	15	16	Ret		17	DNS	19	Ret			Ret	0
											17	0
				Ret								0

Double points were awarded at the Abu Dhabi Grand Prix.

CONSTRUCTORS' CHAMPIONSHIP 2014 (FINAL STANDINGS)

Place	Constructor	Points
1	**Mercedes**	**701**
2	Red Bull-Renault	405
3	Williams-Mercedes	320
4	Ferrari	216
5	McLaren-Mercedes	181
6	Force India	155
7	Toro Rosso-Renault	30
8	Lotus-Renault	10
9	Marussia-Ferrari	2
10	Sauber-Ferrari	0
11	Caterham-Renault	0

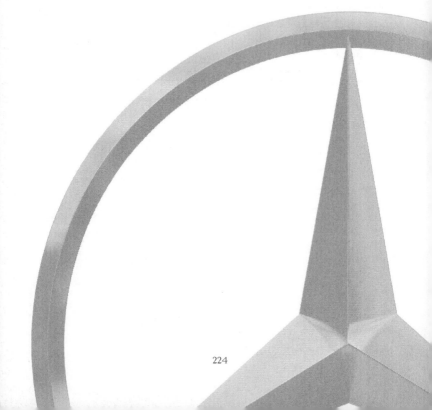

2014 F1 SEASON

EPILOGUE

EPILOGUE

When all the hulla-baloo has died down, there is still the issue of the driver line-up at McLaren for 2015 now that Alonso has been confirmed in the team. At a meeting on December 4th, McLaren couldn't come to a decision whether to retain Button, 34, or Kevin Magnussen, 22. "It's a strange situation but sometimes in life you find yourself in these situations. You just have to deal with it," said Button.

Hamilton, talking on the stage after receiving 2 awards for International Racing Driver of the Year and British Competition Driver, pointed at Button and said, "Jenson, I see you over there, man. I hope you're here next year, dude."

"If it was my first year in F1 it would be a lot more difficult but I've had an amazing career in F1 and to win a world championship and what I've achieved, it's been an amazing experience," Button added. "A couple of months ago it was very tricky but now you just go with it and the last few races have been really enjoyable. I worked with some amazing people at McLaren. It's been a real pleasure to work with those guys."

On December 11th, McLaren finally made their decision and Button was confirmed as Fernando Alonso's team mate for 2015 with an option to extend the contract for 2016. "To be part of McLaren-Honda for more than one year is important. I am not just here to be around for one year. I am here to fight for world championships," Button said. McLaren's exciting new line-up adds more spice to the 2015 season.

At Toro-Rosso, they had already made headlines with the news that the 17 year-old son of ex-Formula 1 driver Jos Verstappen, Max Verstappen was to join them for next year. They've now added 20 year-old Carlos Sainz Jr to their ranks to make up the youngest Formula 1 line-up in history.

Meanwhile, for Champion Lewis Hamilton, the plaudits start flooding in. Sir Stirling Moss, statistically seen as the greatest driver never to win the World Championship, said that Lewis's driving this year made him better than 7 time World Champion Michael Schumacher. "It was a wonderful result for the guy who deserved it," Moss told BBC Radio 5 live. "I'd put him above Schumacher. I mean Schumacher just happened to win a lot of titles, but he wasn't as quick."

On Sunday 14th December Lewis Hamilton was voted the winner of the prestigious BBC Sports Personality of the Year with the pre-award favourite, the golfer Rory McIlroy, as runner-up and athlete Jo Pavey in third. "I was sitting there saying Rory's going to have it," said Hamilton. "I thought it had to be someone else." Hamilton won 209,920 (34%) of the 620,932 votes phoned in by the BBC's audience, with McIlroy getting 123,745 (20%) and Pavey 99,913 (16%). "I want to say a huge thank you to all the people who called in, I really wasn't expecting it. I am so speechless. I'm so proud and honoured to be among such great sporting talent." Hamilton was runner-up to boxer Joe Calzaghe in 2007 and cyclist Sir Chris Hoy the following year, the year of Hamilton's first World title. He was presented with the trophy by former Scotland and Liverpool player Kenny Dalglish after his name was announced by former England rugby player Jonny Wilkinson in front of an audience of 12,000 in Glasgow's SSE Hydro Centre.

According to Sir Jackie Stewart, Lewis Hamilton cannot be considered a great yet, but he is on the right path. Hamilton joins Jackie Stewart (1969, 1971 and 1973), Jim Clark (1963 and 1965) and Graham Hill (1962 and 1968) as the only British drivers to win 2 titles or more.

The 75 year old Jackie Stewart, told BBC Sport that, "Lewis can become one of the great drivers. But you can't judge that based purely on this year's performance because of Mercedes' superiority throughout the whole season. There's a lot still to be done to achieve the greatness that I think everyone has perhaps placed on him prematurely. But he's a young man, so he has many more years in the sport and I think we are going to see even greater things from him. To become a great, Lewis has to continue to win. He must choose the best teams to drive for and keep his head focused on being a professional."

List of top Formula 1 Driver's Championship winners: Michael Schumacher with 7, Juan Manuel Fangio with 5, Alain Prost and Sebastian Vettel on 4, Jack Brabham, Sir Jackie Stewart, Niki Lauda, Nelson Piquet, Ayrton Senna on 3, Alberto Ascari, Graham Hill, Jim Clark, Emerson Fittipaldi, Mika Hakkinen, Fernando Alonso, Lewis Hamilton on 2.

"There are a lot of distractions which come with success and earning that kind of money and that threatens long term success," continued Stewart. " But Lewis made the right decision to leave McLaren and join Mercedes and that is what has brought him the World Championship. Without question, Mercedes is the team to be with," said Stewart. "It's a very good team of people. If they keep the advantage they have enjoyed this season, I see no reason why Hamilton can't win the title next year and thereafter. It's made it slightly dull this year. Everyone expected Mercedes to win the races. Complete domination by any particular make of car is always boring for the spectators. Fans would like to see more competition and I think next year there will be more competition. Honda are coming in to provide engines for McLaren, while Williams will hope to build on their tremendous performance this season and Red Bull will come back strong."

Lewis Hamilton says winning his 2nd world title is the start of "something special" for himself and Mercedes. He joined Mercedes in 2013 after Niki Lauda promised they would make him world champion. Hamilton, said, "I wanted to be part of something building and growing. I feel this is just the beginning. What this team has put together is something incredibly special. We've got great people in their right positions and me and Nico will continue to push the team forward. As will the boss of Mercedes, who has been so committed to building the best engine. These guys know just as much as I do, it's been phenomenal this year. It's really important the steps we take moving forwards to continue improving and I one hundred percent believe the team will do that. I definitely don't feel I am looking for a new challenge. We have a year to go, so there's no particular rush but this is my home and I'm very happy here."

Niki Lauda added, "I asked him to leave McLaren and come to Mercedes and he said 'when are we going to be competitive'. I said I could guarantee him a world championship and in the second year, here it is." On Hamilton's contract talks he said, "We are going to do this in the next two weeks. He's happy, we're happy, I don't see any issues."

"It means so much more than the first one - it feels so long. I feel so blessed." Hamilton added. "It has been an incredible year. It feels like an out-of-body experience. It is very hard to soak all this up. I didn't sleep. I went to bed at 12, woke up 5am, went for a run and thought for sure I would be tired when I got to the race but I felt composed. My family came and surprised me at breakfast. I had wanted them to be here but I didn't know if I would be able to give them time. I didn't want to get to the end and say, 'I wish I had done this or that'."

Hamilton's father, Anthony, step-mother Linda, brother Nicolas and girlfriend Nicole Scherzinger all flew into Abu Dhabi on Sunday morning to surprise him. "It's really going to take some time to sink in. I don't know what I have next week but I hope to see family. At the end of the week we will have a seat fitting but I might need a bit of bulking! I don't really drink so I will let everyone else get obliterated.

After Rosberg's mechanical woes in the last race, Hamilton was aware that the same could happen to him. "As a driver you are always conscious of the possibilities of the car failure," he said. "It's not something you can prevent. We've had ups and downs and I did not know what was going to happen. But I had so much faith. I knew I could do it. I had faith God would keep it going. I had no idea my family and Nicole were coming. I was messaging my dad last night and knew I had to be so selfish and did not want to involve them. But my dad messaged me. I said I wanted them here but either way I knew they would be. I did not hear anything Prince Harry said. It was very cool, I'm very grateful. It's unreal, it's incredible."

Hamilton admitted for the first time that he disliked the double points system. In the post-race news conference, with Williams' driver Felipe Massa, Hamilton said: "Coming to the last race knowing it was double points. Jeez..." He turned to Massa, who he beat to the 2008 title by one point after passing Timo Glock's Toyota at the last corner of the last lap in Brazil, the last race of the season, and said: "Did you think it was a good idea? I didn't think it was a good idea." Massa retorted. "I think it was a good idea in 2008."

Printed in Great Britain
by Amazon.co.uk, Ltd.,
Marston Gate.